I0492189

Also by Tim Burningham

Be An Awesome Boss! The Four C's Model to Leadership Success

How Leaders Can Strengthen Their Organization's Culture

The
Wisdom
Story

How to Create a High-Performing Company Culture and Transform Results

Tim Burningham

A *TAB* Original
Houston, Texas

Copyright ©2020 by Tim Burningham

PO BOX 5156
Houston, TX 77325

Distributed by The Awesome Boss LLC

For ordering information or special discounts for bulk purchases, please contact The Awesome Boss LLC at PO Box 5156, Houston, TX, 77325, or, betheawesomeboss@gmail.com.

Library of Congress Cataloging-In-Publication Data

Burningham, Tim.

The wisdom story : how to create a high-performing company culture and transform results / Tim Burningham.
p. cm.

Issued also as an ebook.

ISBN: 9798699676804

    1.   Company Culture 2. Leadership effectiveness 3. Business I. Title

Printed in the United States of America

First Edition

TAB 04 09 11 03 09 20 02

Contents

This book is dedicated to all the remarkable health care leaders and workers who have made so many personal sacrifices and provided endless amounts of care to those in need during the global coronavirus pandemic.

Your dedication and service to others will not be forgotten.

Introduction

Company culture has become a popular term in recent years. While the importance of culture is not lost on most leaders, understanding how to truly create a culture that has the impact leaders and organizations desire has proved to be tricky.

Media coverage about what makes a culture great has perpetuated the problem and is often shallow and shortsighted. Tales of ping-pong tables and gyms near every break room, unlimited stockpiles of food and beverages, or a seemingly never-ending number of employee perks and benefits makes even the most optimistic leaders skeptical about how to create a strong organizational culture.

Ironically, what does make a company culture great is rarely mentioned, especially in the media. This is probably because the elements that make up a high-performing company culture aren't all that interesting or sophisticated. They don't require specialized knowledge, extensive expertise, or even lots of cash. Instead they are basic, well-known, and even (gasp) practical leadership practices. Consequently, they don't make for good news stories. And thus, leaders and organizations waste their precious time and resources again and again on things that don't work, or they simply ignore their culture problems altogether, unsure of what to do.

The Wisdom Story was written to dispel these myths and bring to light what truly works in building a high-performing company culture. It is also written specifically for leaders who are serious about running and leading successful teams and organizations in a way that is both inspiring and enduring.

The book contains a tale about the incredible transformation of a struggling business. It's an account of an unwavering commitment to proven principles that, when practiced, produce remarkable results. It's a leadership fable about resiliency, courage, and dedication to focusing on what matters most to achieve success.

Finally, it's an inspiring story that reminds us all that any leader in any industry facing any circumstance can achieve results and build an incredible legacy of lasting success when committed to the right things.

Though this leadership fable follows just one leader in one organization, the reality is that there have been many wisdom stories throughout time. If you look hard enough, you will find them.

The Wisdom Story is a companion to the author's earlier book entitled "Be An Awesome Boss! The Four C's Model to Leadership Success."

The Fable

The Offer

"No way!" Grace said emphatically as she looked over at her boss, Dan.

Though she wasn't one to shy away from a challenge, Grace knew Wisdom Health Care Center was a sinking ship, and she wasn't about to jump onboard as captain.

"If anyone can do it, you can. I have no doubt," Dan responded, sounding sincere.

Though known for her confidence, Grace was feeling really uneasy about the conversation she found herself in with her boss, mentor, and friend.

"And how many CEOs has the company gone through over there in the last couple of years? I can think of several off the top of my head."

"Yes, there have been many over the years, but none has been Grace Holden. You've been preparing for this chance for a while now. It's always been your goal to become a CEO for our company. I know you're ready for this."

Though Dan was right that it was something she had been looking forward to for a long time, Grace had never expected to become the CEO of a health care center that had such a poor reputation and was so widely known as a bad performer.

Wiser Care, Inc., the company Grace had worked for over the last seven years, owned health care centers across the country, and Wisdom Health Care Center had been among the worst performers for years. From financial struggles to clinical issues, Wisdom was a health care center most people wanted to run from.

"Plus, since it's just on the other side of town, you won't have to move your family across the country like a lot of CEOs do when given their first opportunity to be in charge of a center. I know Eric and the girls will appreciate that."

Though Grace knew her husband and two young daughters would be happy to hear they wouldn't have to move, she wasn't convinced this was the right career move for her.

"No matter what opportunity you get, Grace, more likely than not, it will be at a health care center that is struggling. That's just the way it is."

"But Wisdom?" Grace questioned. She knew Dan was right, but she wouldn't exactly classify Wisdom as a health care center that was simply struggling. *Hopeless* seemed like a more appropriate word to describe it.

"Look, rarely does a CEO just walk away from a good situation and hand it over to someone else. Most first-time CEOs at Wiser Care, Inc. have to prove themselves by taking on a challenging position that has been vacated by a leader who wasn't able to pull the right levers to help it succeed."

Again, Grace didn't disagree with what Dan was saying. She knew she would have to take on a challenge. But Wisdom was more than a challenge. *It's more like a death sentence*, she thought to herself incredulously.

"The way I look at it," Dan now said, easing back in his chair, "Wisdom can only improve under your leadership. With expectations as low as they are over there, you really can't lose. And if—" Dan paused for a moment as if contemplating what he was about to say. "And *when* you turn it around, you'll be a rock star in our company. Heck, you'll be a rock star in the entire industry. I know you can do it, Grace."

Grace had always believed she'd never forget the day she was finally offered the opportunity to become a CEO. She realized now she had been right, but the reason she wouldn't forget this day was all wrong. Instead of being elated, she was confused and, quite frankly, somewhat frightened.

One reason was that Wisdom and Northfield, the health care center where she was currently working under Dan as his COO, could not have been more different. Yes, both were owned by Wiser Care, Inc., and yes, both were health care centers that provided similar health care services, but other than that, the two didn't have much in common.

For example, Northfield had a long history of success and was led by an experienced, long-standing CEO, while Wisdom was a center that had consistently poor results for years, exacerbated by a revolving door of leadership, including the CEO position. Northfield was a perennial award winner with stellar outcomes and laudable service excellence, while Wisdom had never won any award in its history to Grace's knowledge. Northfield had stable, long-tenured staff and a strong workplace culture, and Wisdom clearly did not.

Though owned by the same company, the two health care centers could not have been further apart in terms of reputation, stability, and performance. So, although Grace had set her sights on becoming a CEO ever since joining Wiser Care, Inc., she had never imagined it could be at a place as loathed as Wisdom Health Care Center.

They must think I'm crazy to consider such an offer, Grace reasoned to herself as she left Dan's office.

Conflicted

"That's fantastic news, Grace," her husband, Eric, told her that evening as she shared what had happened at work earlier in the day. "It's been a long time coming. We should celebrate."

Grace was amused her husband was so confident and excited about the opportunity because she certainly did not feel the same. She knew he didn't fully comprehend what she would be getting herself into if she accepted the position. For that reason, she was not actually considering it. Still, his enthusiasm reminded her of what her goal had always been and where she still hoped to end up some day.

"The fact that we don't have to move is a huge blessing for our family. There is no way you can pass this up, right?" Eric asked.

In the back of her mind, Grace had been fighting back against this one incredibly attractive piece of the offer since learning about it. But just because becoming a CEO and not having to move were exactly what she and her family had always wanted, it didn't mean this specific opportunity was the right one for her.

Still, with Wisdom Health Care Center located just across town, it would mean her husband could keep the job he enjoyed in the IT field, and her daughters could stay in their same schools and activities. The Holden family all loved where they lived and had made many close friends over the years. And although becoming a successful CEO was Grace's ultimate career goal, its one drawback had always been the idea of where they would end up someday. The simple fact that they most likely would have to uproot their little family to advance her career had always been a concern.

"It does sound like a big challenge, sugar, but if anyone can do it, you can. You know the girls and I will have your back one hundred percent."

Grace sighed and tried to fight back the feelings and thoughts she had inside. On the one hand, Wisdom was an ideal setup; it allowed her and her family to essentially have what they all wanted.

On the other hand, it was full of risk. Accepting the position had the potential to hurt her career and would more than likely overtake her personal and family life, at least for a while. And if things didn't work out, it could possibly derail everything they believed they had gained by taking the position. Then again, an opportunity like this might never present itself again, and she might regret passing it up for years to come.

"Maybe I need to give this some serious consideration," Grace finally said, almost to herself. She was more than annoyed to notice how excited her husband seemed.

Grace and her husband sat in silence for a few more moments before Eric finally said, "Besides, think about how much you will bless the lives of all those people over there. They need a good leader like you to make it a great place. This is why you got into health care, right? To help people. They probably have never had a good CEO. You could change that for them."

"You sound like Dan," Grace said, feeling frustrated and not trying to hide it. *He really doesn't understand,* Grace thought, shaking her head.

Consideration

Ever since Grace had decided to take a more serious look at the Wisdom opportunity, she had been fervently reviewing the health care center's financial reports. She noticed that not only were expenses at Wisdom extremely high, but revenue was also at an all-time low in recent months. Both of these seemed like good indicators that there was real potential for better performance over there.

After comparing Wisdom's financial reports with Northfield's, Grace easily identified a lot of opportunities she felt would allow her to improve the financial footing at Wisdom rather quickly. This boosted her interest.

Grace also realized another advantage she had going for her: for the last four and a half years, she had worked under one of the most successful CEOs at Wiser Care, Inc. Dan "The Man" Rosier, as most people affectionately called him, had taught her a lot, not only about the industry but also about how to create a great culture and lead a high-performing team. She recognized that she had been prepared better than perhaps anyone else in the company to tackle the challenges Wisdom might present.

Finally, the thought that Dan believed in her abilities and would be close by to offer support whenever needed was reassuring. She had little doubt he would do whatever he could to help her succeed.

All this added to Grace's growing belief that she just might be the right woman for the job and the one leader in the company who could turn things around at Wisdom.

* * *

Late that evening, as Grace settled into bed next to her husband, who was already breathing deeply, she thought again about the many CEOs she had met or heard about over the years who had come and gone at Wisdom. Each had only been able to achieve marginal improvements and fleeting success. Though these thoughts made her feel nervous all over again, Grace believed in her own abilities. In the stillness of the night, she felt a quiet confidence that she could turn around the long history of poor performance at Wisdom.

Acceptance

"I'm going to take it," Grace said with less enthusiasm than she had wanted to have in the moment. Though she had concluded that accepting the offer was the right thing for her to do, it didn't take away from her feelings of uneasiness about the unsteady operation she'd be walking into.

"Great!" Dan said, adding, "I'm not surprised. I've never seen you back down from a challenge. I'm confident you can do this."

As Grace walked out of Dan's office, the full realization that her opportunity to become CEO of a health care center hit her, and she felt a jolt of exhilaration. Though there were reasons to worry, she was confident she could do it. She also knew she was ready to take this exciting step in her blossoming career.

At least that's what she thought…

Rumors

Grace's last few weeks at Northfield had flown by, and she was now feeling more optimistic than ever about her impending first day at Wisdom. She felt certain she fully understood the magnitude of the difficulties she would soon be facing and knew she was ready to meet them head-on. Not only was the health care center losing money, but its poor reputation and poor quality of care had been weighing down the entire organization for years, and she was going to change that.

Pulling into her driveway, arriving home a little earlier than normal after her last day of work at Northfield, Grace felt her phone vibrating in her pocket. Pulling it out quickly, she saw it was a text message from Tom asking if she could talk.

Tom Hernandez, the COO of Wiser Care, Inc. was a short, balding gentleman with a booming voice and often stern demeanor. Grace knew Tom had joined the company in the early days and had worked his way up to the position he now held. To her, he seemed to have a good knowledge of the industry, and he knew the company's history inside and out and talked about it often. Despite his somewhat intimidating persona, which turned some people off, Grace believed he was a likeable guy and looked forward to working more closely with him in her new role.

Though she had met Tom on several occasions and had spoken to him about the CEO position at Wisdom, she wasn't used to receiving messages directly from him yet.

For whatever reason, she felt a little on edge as she gave him a call.

After some expected pleasantries, Tom suddenly sounded more serious.

"I have some news I need to share with you. Though I really wanted to tell you this in person, I felt the sooner I let you know the better."

By the tone of Tom's voice, Grace knew something must be wrong. *Am I not getting the job after all?* she worried. The next part of their conversation was somewhat of a blur.

First, Tom said something about just leaving a meeting with the board of directors and then added a bit about a lot of discussion and debate over what to do with Wisdom. Finally, he shared, "A decision has been made that will affect you, Grace."

At that moment, Grace knew that what Tom was about to say would completely change things for her.

"If you don't make substantial progress at Wisdom over the next six months, then the company will be selling the asset. I'm sorry to have to share this with you on the eve of your first day."

Wondering if she might be dreaming, Grace questioned in her mind, *How can this be?*

Though she had heard an occasional rumor that the company wanted to sell the Wisdom Health Care Center, Grace had always brushed it aside as unfounded gossip, especially since the center had been losing money consistently for so many years, and nothing ever seemed to happen.

The realization of Tom's words suddenly felt like a punch in the gut as Grace tried to grasp the implications of it all.

"I tried to ask for at least one more year with a brand-new CEO starting and all, but to make a long story short, I wasn't successful."

Grace tried to pull herself together and say something but wasn't sure how to respond.

She finally forced out a barely audible "OK." And then, after a moment, she added, "So what does this mean for my future should the health care center be sold?"

The rest of their conversation was even more foggy because, at that point, Grace's mind was spinning, though she remembered Tom had assured her that regardless of what happened at Wisdom Health Care Center, he would take personal responsibility for finding her a good permanent place at another center within the organization. Of course, there were no promises made about what position or where in the country it might be.

When Grace finally hung up her phone, she first felt shocked and then angry. Finally, she felt sick to her stomach all over again. *Six months? That's it? Wisdom is a mess. It would be impossible for even a seasoned CEO to turn that place around in six months.*

Should I back out and refuse to start tomorrow? But where would I go? I've already trained my replacement at Northfield, and that wouldn't be fair to him. Or to the people at Wisdom.

How can Wiser Care do this? This isn't right!

As if the pressure to rescue a struggling operation hadn't already been enough, Grace now took in the full gravity of the situation she would be walking into beginning tomorrow morning.

Reality Check

It was the end of her first day on the job as CEO at Wisdom Health Care Center, and Grace was already feeling exhausted. In nearly every possible way, things were worse than she had even imagined. She had spent her entire first day dealing with what felt like an endless number of urgent problems, complaints, and issues.

Although Grace had been aware Wisdom was losing money and had a poor reputation in the community, what she hadn't anticipated was the lack of depth on her team: that is to say, the lack of a team at all.

Grace learned early in her day that the center was using a contracting registry to supply nursing staff to provide care to the patients. In her fifteen years of experience in the industry, she had never seen or heard of a center staffed like Wisdom was. Sure, some health care centers she had worked for had used contracted clinicians and caregivers from time to time, but typically, it was only for a few hard-to-fill shifts and not 70 percent of all shifts during the day.

Grace was stunned by this unexpected staffing crisis and regretted she had not figured it out while analyzing the center's financial reports. She knew contracted staff was not only expensive, but it also increased the likelihood of poor customer service and poor clinical care. Grace felt deeply troubled by this unanticipated challenge.

As if this discovery of limited staff wasn't bad enough, Grace's meeting with her VP of clinical services early that afternoon didn't bring the slightest amount of hope that the problem would be resolved anytime soon. In fact, when Grace had asked him about the staffing crisis, he had nonchalantly commented that it made each day "an adventure" before admitting the situation was out of control.

Grace then thought about what she had done next and how it had caused her to fall further into despair. After leaving her VP of clinical services' office she had marched right over to the office of her VP of HR, Rosie. Asking to see any applications they had on hand, she soon discovered there were only a few and most weren't even qualified for the positions they were applying for.

Rosie had quickly shared what she had tried to do to attract talent, but explained it seemed that anyone who knew about the reputation of the health care center did not want to work there.

Unfortunately, Grace felt she was beginning to uncover a lot of reasons why.

Grace felt certain the staffing crisis exacerbated the care complaints, low customer satisfaction results, and poor customer retention rates. She knew instantly that one of her top priorities had to be improving the staffing situation as quickly as possible, but how?

The thrill she had felt starting as the CEO at Wisdom seemed like a distant memory at this point. Grace was beginning to wonder what she had gotten herself into.

* * *

By the end of Grace's first week, things had gone from bad to worse. As Grace tried to establish some stability in staffing, she couldn't help but question the efforts of many members of her leadership team. *How could they have let it get so bad here, and why hadn't they done more to keep employees around?* These were the types of questions she had asked herself and others over and over again throughout the week, without many reasonable answers.

Grace knew she had let the stress of the situation get the best of her already, and she regretted having behaved poorly toward some of her team members at times during the week. By her estimation, the health care center was a much bigger mess than she had ever imagined it could possibly be. And the fact she had only six months to turn things around didn't help with the extreme pressure she was feeling.

Just when Grace believed things couldn't get any worse, they did.

Bad to Worse

Unexpectedly, within forty-eight hours of each other, three of Grace's top leaders walked out the door, leaving her and the rest of her tattered team to fend for themselves.

The first to go was the VP of clinical services, who stated that Grace was trying to harm patients by controlling staffing levels too much. He threatened that the center would fall apart without him.

A few moments later, the second in command over the clinical services department, the director of nursing services, resigned. And although she didn't offer the same threats as her boss had, she did sarcastically wish Grace good luck.

The sudden departure of the top two clinical leaders left the largest and most important department within her health care center basically leaderless. Grace worried care would continue to deteriorate.

The next person to go was a much bigger surprise. Just a day after the top two clinical leaders had resigned, Grace's VP of marketing informed her he was quitting to go work for a nearby competitor. As if this wasn't bad enough, he also told Grace he was leaving immediately because his new employer desperately needed him to start right away.

With this latest departure, Grace began to feel like she was riding in the cockpit of a speeding plane headed straight for the ground. Though she wanted to take control of the situation and save the rest of her team and everyone else who depended on the health care center from a devastating crash landing, she wasn't sure she knew how. For a few moments, Grace felt not only helpless but also hopeless.

After taking a moment, Grace pulled herself together and knew she had to focus on things within her control.

First, she went to work making contingency plans to cover for the departed clinical leaders, including shifting the remaining nurse supervisors to focus on orientating and training new staff. She also asked a few other department leaders to chip in to help with staffing and documentation and asked Rosie to assume the role of recruiting and hiring all personnel in the nursing department.

Feeling slightly better with a short-term plan in place to provide adequate care, she then turned her attention to marketing. She talked to a few different department heads about marketing efforts and asked for their support to fill in with some vital roles and tasks. She also decided that she would assume primary responsibility for the center's relationship with their most important referral sources and contacts.

With a slight sense of stability reestablished, Grace tried not to think about how soon things might spiral out of control again.

SOS

It was now early Saturday morning, and Grace had gotten little sleep since starting at Wisdom. She felt drained.

In the middle of the night, Grace had decided she couldn't wait any longer and texted her former boss and mentor, Dan. It came as no surprise to her that he was willing to meet as soon as she wanted, even offering to convene in the middle of the night. Though Grace was tempted to take Dan up on his offer, they agreed on 7:30 a.m. in his office.

As she arrived at Northfield, Grace realized she'd never expected to be pulling into the familiar parking lot again so soon. She felt a quick twinge of disappointment and some embarrassment.

Walking toward the front door, Grace had a slight sense of regret that she had chosen to leave such a comfortable position at such a great place.

As she passed through the familiar halls, she felt she was back home. Her first ten days as CEO at Wisdom had been a disaster. Despite the difficulties she had encountered, though, Grace knew she was resilient and that she had overcome difficult challenges before. She had little doubt she'd eventually make things a lot better at Wisdom.

As she knocked on Dan's office door, she reminded herself that he wasn't someone who was going to judge her unfairly or think poorly of her. She needed to lay it all out on the table if she wanted his best advice.

Most importantly, Grace was certain Dan would provide sound guidance and insights on how she could get her health care center out of the mess it currently found itself in.

The Four *C*'s Model

Following a warm welcome from Dan, Grace explained what was going on at her center. After about twenty-five minutes of nonstop talking, Grace realized she hadn't let Dan speak at all and began feeling a bit sheepish.

Perhaps he thinks I'm not up to the challenge after all, Grace thought, suddenly feeling uneasy. She didn't want Dan to be disappointed in her. Just as she was searching for something positive to say, Dan broke his silence.

"I think we need to review the four *C*'s model to creating a high-performing culture again," he said, flashing a smile. Grace knew he had listened patiently to her and, like always, she felt his genuine concern. But now with what seemed like a flip of a switch, he was looking too enthused based on the desperate situation she had just laid out in front of him. Then again, having worked with Dan for many years, his positive demeanor wasn't surprising to her as that was the way he nearly always behaved.

Grace knew all about the four *C*'s model, and she had observed Dan get excited about it on many occasions in the past. Each time he talked about it, he seemed to get this surge of energy that became infectious. Perhaps it was because he knew from experience it worked. At least it seemed to have worked for Dan in his situation. *My situation is so different, though*, Grace thought as she braced herself to hear the familiar lecture.

"The four *C*'s model represents the most important steps a leader should take in any given situation. They are the steps for creating an exceptional culture. Culture shapes performance and results. And by the sound of it, an improvement in culture by applying the four *C*'s is exactly what will help you resolve your problems."

Grace wasn't so sure about that but didn't want to question him right away as he continued.

"Following the model and applying the principles at your health care center are the most critical things you can do if you want to be a successful leader and turn things around. I know it will help you with all the challenges you are facing."

Grace had heard this four *C*'s lecture many times before and worried Dan hadn't grasped what she had shared. In her situation, the model didn't really seem to apply because the problems at Wisdom Health Care Center seemed different—they were too big and challenging and overwhelming for the four *C*'s to help. And they had started gushing into her office like water from an open fire hose the moment she had walked through the door on her first day.

With all that was going on at Wisdom, Grace didn't believe she had the capacity or the time for the four *C*'s model lecture. She was swimming in problems she was certain the four *C*'s model couldn't fix.

"You already know what has helped me to be successful throughout my career," Dan continued. "Without this framework or model, I'd be just as lost as you seem to be right now."

Dan flashed his contagious smile again. Grace felt discouraged about where the conversation was going. "I know you've heard my speech about this model over and over again, but I'd like to review it with you one more time if you will allow me to."

Grace hesitated. *Do I really have time for this?* she thought. She sat for another moment thinking about what to say but then suddenly felt ashamed. She knew on a personal level about Dan's success as a leader and the incredible health care center he was running using the four *C*'s model. Grace had witnessed firsthand that it worked; she had lived it, yet she was now questioning everything she had learned.

Feeling guilty about being irritated that Dan was bringing up the model, she was determined to pay closer attention to his explanation than she ever had before. She sat up in her chair, mustered a smile, and said sarcastically, "I guess I'll allow it just this one last time."

Dan smiled back, nodded, and stood. "I was beginning to think you were going to turn me down."

With her mind made up to listen intently, Grace followed Dan with her eyes as he walked over to the whiteboard at the far end of his office. She sat quietly as he drew out what she recognized as the familiar base of the four *C*'s model. This is how it looked.

"The base of the model is clarity. You must establish clarity first to build the right culture at Wisdom and to eventually be successful."

Grace nodded her head and was feeling a bit more enthusiastic, probably because of Dan's oozing passion for what he was sharing.

"You've got to start here, Grace. This is your foundation. Without a high level of organizational clarity throughout your health care center, you'll never get out of that mess over there. Clarity must demand most of your attention in the beginning."

Grace considered that comment as Dan added three bullet points below the diagram.

"You have to concentrate on building clarity around these specific items first," Dan said, now pointing to what he had added on the whiteboard, which she knew well. This is how it now looked.

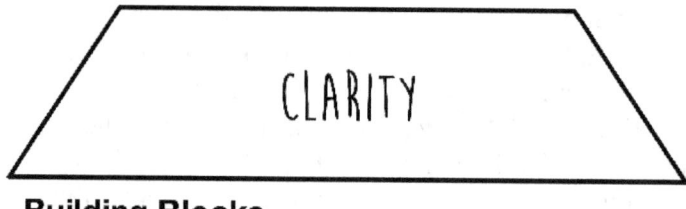

Building Blocks
- Mission
- Vision
- Values

Dan paused for another moment as if to make sure Grace was listening and then continued. "Clarity aligns a team, builds trust, and removes so many problems that come along with ambiguity and uncertainty in the workplace. People need to be clear about the purpose of their work, where they are going, and what standards they should be striving to live—or, in other words, the mission, vision, and values. These are the building blocks to a great culture.

"Do you believe any of this is clear to your people at Wisdom?"

Grace felt her cheeks begin to turn red. It was obvious it wasn't clear, and she had done little to improve the confusion that existed at Wisdom around what Dan believed were the most important items to make clear. She could tell Dan knew the answer already without her saying anything.

"When clarity is lacking, it can be hard for the team to engage and do their best work. Your employees want to be in the know. They want to know what the plan is and what matters most to their company. You can give that to them." Dan paused for a moment before saying, "Let me rephrase that. As their leader, you *should* give that to them because you're the only one that can. Providing clarity as a leader is your most important role."

Grace had enjoyed how clear things had been working with Dan. Everyone always seemed to be on the same page—they all knew what the expectations were and what goals they were striving to achieve. They also knew their progress toward those goals and where they needed to improve. Grace realized clarity kept everyone focused on the same important things and produced incredible unity and cohesion. She felt it had been a major reason for their team's success at Northfield.

"So to turn things around and build a strong culture, you first need to make the building blocks super clear over there."

Grace nodded, copying down the diagram in a notebook she had brought.

"Once the building blocks are clear, you should then begin to focus on making other important items clear. I like to call these big-ticket items."

Dan paused again to add to what he had already written on the whiteboard.

```
                 ┌─────────────────────────────────┐
                /                                     \
               /          CLARITY                      \
              /                                          \
             └────────────────────────────────────────────┘
```

Building Blocks

- Mission
- Vision
- Values

Big-Ticket Items

- Roles & Responsibilities
- Evaluation Process
- Standards & Expectations
- Goals
- Results
- "The Why" (for meetings, systems, procedures, policies, decisions, etc.)

"Without organizational clarity around these most important items, it will be hard to have much success over there, especially based on the current state of the operation and its history. Creating clarity will help your people perform better. Clarity is vital to turning the culture and results around at Wisdom."

As Grace looked over the building blocks and big-ticket items Dan had written on the board, she knew there was little clarity surrounding most of them at Wisdom.

"Do you remember the most important tool for creating clarity?" Dan asked.

She thought for a moment, a little confused about what exactly he was asking, and then she realized she had the answer. "It's repetition."

"That's right," Dan said with a smile. "Other than living by what you say, of course, in order to effectively create clarity, you must become comfortable repeating the same messages often.

"Where most leaders and organizations fail with clarity is they believe they have been clear when the truth is they haven't been. For example, they may say something once or twice and then expect everyone to remember it and get it. This isn't realistic. People need to hear a message multiple times before they begin to grasp it and truly believe in it. And then once they do grasp it, that message needs to be repeated again and again for people to continue to embrace it."

Grace nodded and Dan continued.

"And remember, there is a big difference between *sort of* clear and *really* clear. To build a high-performing culture at Wisdom, these items must become really clear. This is the only way to create the levels of organizational clarity you will need to run a successful operation over there."

Dan was a model of repeating himself often. In fact, on several occasions, Grace had stopped him mid-sentence and completed his thought for him because she knew exactly what he was about to say. He always seemed to enjoy that. Grace thought about the chances of that ever happening to her at Wisdom.

"The next step in the model is consistency," Dan continued, pulling Grace from her thoughts. He then turned and added to what he had already written on the board. This included adding another layer to the pyramid as well as some bullet points off to the side of the second layer.

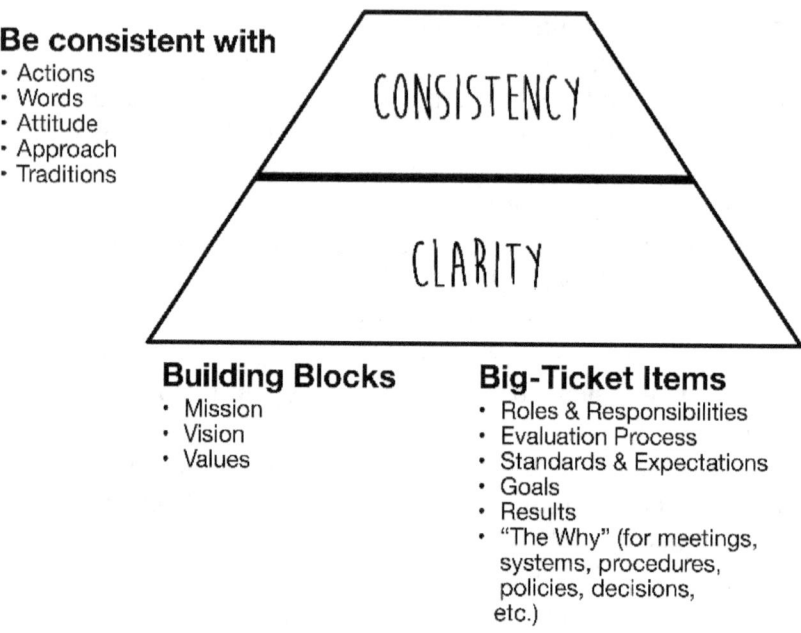

Be consistent with
- Actions
- Words
- Attitude
- Approach
- Traditions

CONSISTENCY

CLARITY

Building Blocks
- Mission
- Vision
- Values

Big-Ticket Items
- Roles & Responsibilities
- Evaluation Process
- Standards & Expectations
- Goals
- Results
- "The Why" (for meetings, systems, procedures, policies, decisions, etc.)

"Consistency at your center will create stability. Just like being in the know is important, employees crave a level of certainty they can count on at work."

Grace agreed that consistency was also something that had a tremendous impact on the results at Northfield and was lacking at Wisdom.

"In a way, clarity is your message, and consistency is your action around that message. If you claim a core value is one thing but then you do another, this creates uncertainty and hurts trust. You must be consistent in what you say, in what you do, in how you behave, and in how you approach similar situations."

Grace nodded as she thought about her somewhat erratic behavior over the last week and a half at Wisdom. She had forgotten how angry she could become when she was totally stressed out. She had justified her actions because she believed people were being neglectful and weren't completing what she perceived to be the basics of their jobs. She realized she needed to be more consistent with her attitude and actions in addition to making things more clear.

"Things are bound to change rapidly while you're there." Dan paused for a second and added, "Heck, things have to change in order to improve. But, you still need to focus on being consistent with things you can control, such as your actions, words, attitude, and approach. Consistency takes discipline but will create a sense of stability for your team, something that has been lacking at Wisdom over the years, no question."

Grace decided to jump in and take a more active role in the discussion. "I agree. Consistency has been lacking at Wisdom. Employee turnover alone has caused a very volatile work environment. This second step will take time and effort to establish over there, and I'm afraid I haven't helped with it much yet. I am confident we can get there, though."

"I know you can get there as well," Dan said, sounding reassuring. "Remember, consistency is about establishing predictable patterns and a certain cadence people can come to expect. It's taking a disciplined approach to your thoughts, words, and actions. Consistency will be vital to creating an extraordinary culture in your center."

Grace nodded and believed more consistency could really boost morale at Wisdom.

"The next step or the top of the pyramid is what?" Dan asked with a slight grin.

"Celebration," Grace replied with more enthusiasm than expected.

"That's right," Dan responded, equally excited. "I like to think of celebration as the icing on the cake of a strong company culture."

Dan then turned to the whiteboard and added to his diagram while saying, "Remember, celebration is made up of three important elements. Those are recognition, measurement, and fun."

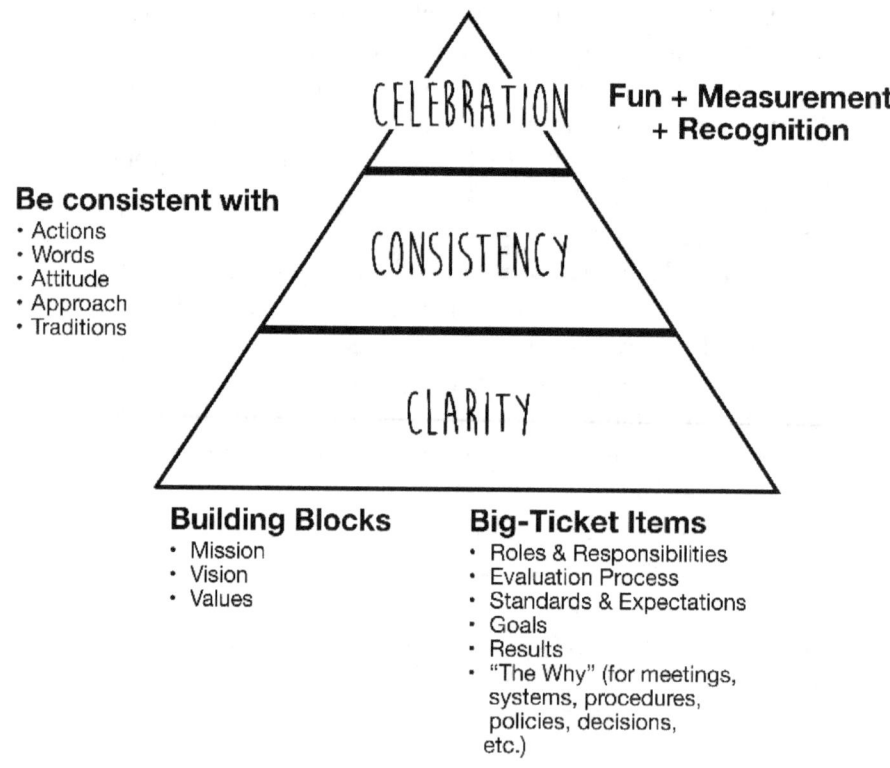

CELEBRATION — **Fun + Measurement + Recognition**

CONSISTENCY

Be consistent with
- Actions
- Words
- Attitude
- Approach
- Traditions

CLARITY

Building Blocks
- Mission
- Vision
- Values

Big-Ticket Items
- Roles & Responsibilities
- Evaluation Process
- Standards & Expectations
- Goals
- Results
- "The Why" (for meetings, systems, procedures, policies, decisions, etc.)

As Dan added the third *C*, Grace felt an unexpected sense of gratitude toward him. He had taught her this repeatedly throughout the years, and being removed from the struggles at Wisdom, it all made sense again.

She was grateful Dan was so patient with her and was reminded of how great it had been working under him.

"You need all three elements of the third C in order to really establish it. Remember, everyone likes to be recognized and feel appreciated. Whether intentional or not, ignoring or failing to acknowledge your people for the contributions they're making will really hurt performance. So don't forget to recognize people often—even for small things."

Grace wasn't sure she had recognized anyone at all yet at Wisdom. She knew this was a problem.

"Also, more than any other C, celebration is about helping people feel connected to each other through fun. When you create a fun atmosphere and things aren't so serious all the time, people bond and build real relationships in ways they never otherwise would. When you focus on celebrating with your team, you can create lasting memories that people will cherish. Just like being in the know and feeling secure are both important at work, so is having a sense of belonging and connection. Humans are wired to connect, and frequent celebration helps us do it in a genuine way."

Grace decided it was time to show she had paid attention over the years and chimed in again. "Celebration is often what we look forward to most in life. We celebrate all the time, whether it's a holiday, birthday, big game, special event, or something else. Celebrations are a big part of our life outside work, so it only makes sense to make them an important part inside work as well."

Dan looked pleased. "I could not have said it better myself. You're good at this, Grace. What else can you tell me about the third C?"

"I've only learned it from the best." Grace smiled. She then thought for a moment before adding, "Though it may be fun to celebrate birthdays, work anniversaries, and holidays at work, it's also critical to celebrate when accomplishments are achieved. A team ought to set clear goals and then consistently measure and track their progress toward meeting those goals. Once they reach them, or even when they are making progress toward them, they need to celebrate."

"That's right," Dan answered enthusiastically. Grace realized again how little she had done in regard to the four C's model during her first days at Wisdom.

"You can't forget this Grace. Your progress may be slow initially, but you need to celebrate any positive progress you make. I'm sure you won't hit your big goals right away. But as you inch toward them, take time to measure your progress, recognize your people, and have fun—or, in other words, celebrate."

Grace decided to add something more that she felt certain would please Dan. "And I won't forget that many mistakenly think adding celebration is about doing something once or twice a year to celebrate, like a big company barbeque or holiday party, but this isn't adequate. Like the other C's in the model, celebration needs to be established at work on a daily basis." Grace knew this was always something Dan worried leaders didn't grasp about the model—that each C, including celebration, could be and should be emphasized, established, and reinforced daily.

Dan smiled wide. "That's right."

Grace and Dan talked more about how she could implement the third C at Wisdom before Dan shifted the conversation.

"The final C is important, and it's not really a step like the others in the model. As I've told you in the past, a leader should begin implementing this C from the first day they begin to lead a team. The reason is this final C acts like a multiplier or amplifier to the other three C's. The efforts you make with the first three steps will be magnified by the presence of this fourth *C*, which you know is charity." Dan turned again and completed the diagram of the four *C*'s model on the whiteboard.

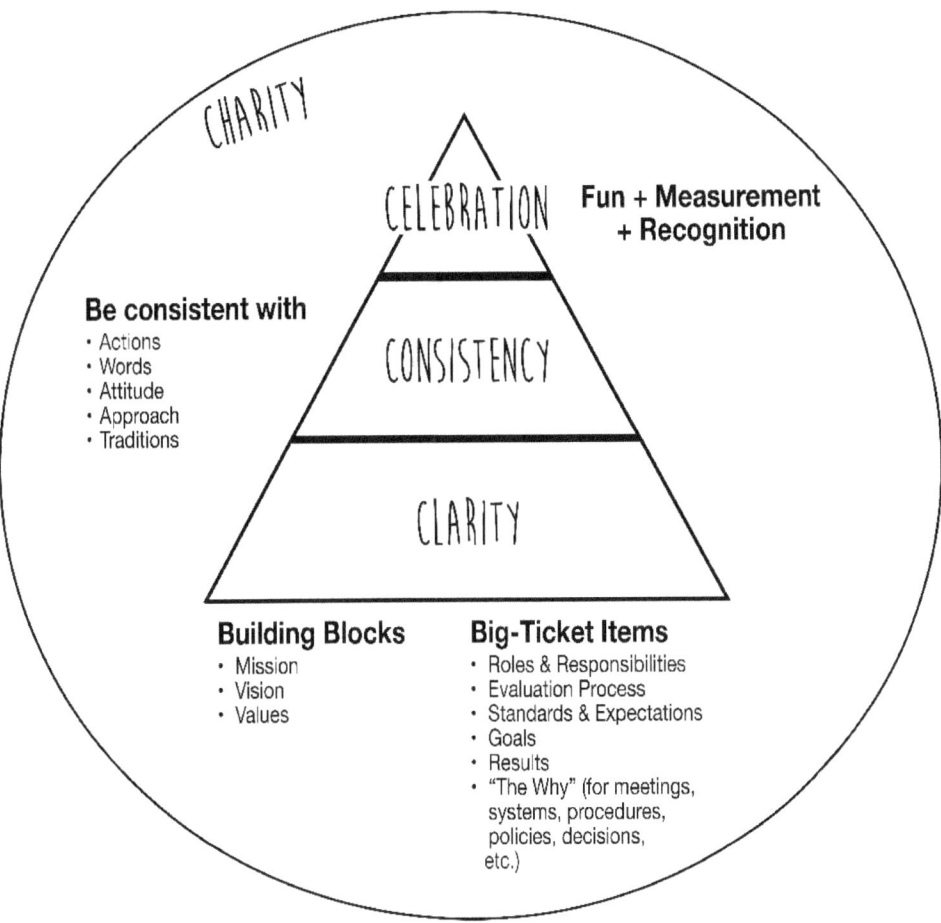

"This last *C* encircles the pyramid to show how it influences your efforts with the other three in the model."

Dan put the cap back on the marker and walked back to his chair.

"Charity is about helping people feel known and cared about at work. People need to feel like valued human beings and not just another number or a product that is expendable or easily replaced."

Grace had always admired this about Dan. He did treat everyone kindly, and he knew something about everyone. It didn't matter if you were a housekeeper or a physician at his health care center; Dan always took interest in you and strived to always treat each person with respect.

"And charity isn't about taking a specific action or another, but rather it's about how. How you take that action. You can take any action with or without charity."

Dan paused for just a moment before continuing, "For example, you can provide clarity with or without charity or consistency with or without charity, and you can even celebrate with charity or without it.

"You get the best results and the best possible outcomes, and you build the best culture when you do things with charity."

Dan sat back in his chair now as if relaxing. "Can you give me an example of what doing something with or without charity may look like?"

Grace had to think only for a second before she had one. "Sure. For example, let's say I have a team member who is chronically missing work, and it is time to give them a written warning for work attendance. I can present this warning with or without charity.

"Without charity, I might present this disciplinary action in a way that demoralizes the person. I might threaten them, blame them, belittle them, yell at them, or be disrespectful in some other way toward them."

Dan was nodding, so Grace continued.

"And the presentation of the disciplinary action might be all about me—how they are making my life miserable

34

and messing things up for me by not showing up. And I probably wouldn't take time to listen to them either or hear them out or even brainstorm possible solutions with them so that they could be successful at work."

Dan looked satisfied with what she had said so far, so she went on.

"With charity, I'd approach the presentation of the written warning much differently. For example, I might explain why it is so important for them to come to work and point out how it affects them as well as others on the team when they don't. I might also ask why they are missing so much work and really take the time to listen to them. I'd maybe even try to understand how I could help them be successful and perhaps brainstorm ideas with them on how they could improve their work attendance.

"With charity, the focus of the meeting would be on them and how I could help them succeed. I'd genuinely want to help them rather than simply going through the necessary steps to eventually separate them from their employment with us."

"That's right—perfect example, Grace. Charity isn't about a certain action to take but rather about how we perform that action. In this instance, a written warning would be the appropriate action to take, but again, you can take it with or without charity."

Dan now looked directly at Grace, adding, "If people don't feel anyone cares about them at work, then your efforts around establishing the other three C's will be greatly diminished. Or when people don't feel like their supervisor knows them at all, and who they are and what makes them unique, then charity levels will become dangerously low, and this will make it much harder to establish the other three C's and be successful."

The two colleagues sat in silence for a moment, then Dan added, "I've been to Wisdom a few times, and I'm certain most team members over there have not felt much charity from their leaders in the past."

Grace had to agree with Dan's comment.

"You've been at the center for over a week now—I'm sure you've made progress with showing charity toward them, right?"

In that moment, Grace suddenly felt more convicted than she could ever recall in her entire life. She knew instantly she hadn't come close to living up to all Dan had taught her over the years. She began feeling extremely uncomfortable.

But I don't have any time to show charity, she thought, trying to justify her actions to herself. She then recognized her thought was simply an excuse. She felt exposed.

Looking back at Dan, Grace realized he was still waiting for her response. She felt her cheeks turning red once again. She knew her hesitation and body language had already given her away.

Before she could stammer out any words, Dan smiled a warm smile and leaned back in his chair, putting his hands behind his head. Grace felt Dan had always shown confidence in her—in fact, she knew his glowing endorsement was probably the biggest reason she was chosen over others to run Wisdom. She suddenly felt remorse for how she had performed as the new CEO at Wisdom over the last week and a half.

I can't believe I have completely ignored this. She had loved the four *C*'s model and believed in it wholeheartedly while working under Dan. But somehow, she had completely dismissed it at Wisdom.

Grace knew she needed to come clean and be open with Dan. She knew it was the only way she would begin to feel better about things.

"Despite all your talks and your example on the importance of the four *C*'s model, I have to admit I haven't thought much about it during my first week and a half at Wisdom." Though she knew Dan recognized this already, it brought relief just saying it out loud.

Dan looked at her, offering, "It's OK. There is still plenty of time to improve. If you focus on each *C* now, you can still have a lot of success over there."

Grace nodded in agreement. After a moment, she said, "I do have a question, although I'm a little embarrassed to ask it."

Dan moved forward in his chair, asking, "What is it?"

"What if I don't feel a lot of charity for my people right now? I mean, I'm really frustrated with them. I can't believe the mess it is in. What do I do?"

Dan now moved back in his chair again, looking as if he was contemplating her question before stating, "Good question. This can be tricky, but I've been there before. I have a thought that I believe will help."

Grace felt both surprised and somewhat relieved to know Dan had felt this way before.

"Over the years, I've learned when I don't feel a lot of charity toward someone, I need to spend more time really getting to know them. Each time I've put forth a sincere effort to get to know my people on a personal level, to dig deep and learn their story and what makes them tick, I've come to care more about them."

Grace nodded, realizing she had done little to get to know her team at Wisdom. In fact, she could think of very little she actually knew about them outside work.

"I hope that helps."

"It does," Grace responded.

Dan then said, "The more quickly you can establish clarity, consistency, celebration, and charity, the faster Wisdom will begin to turn around. Remember, start with clarity first, then turn your attention to consistency, and then on to celebration while showing charity throughout the entire process. Building up these four *C*'s at Wisdom will take time, but in them lies your key to success. The four *C*'s model is how you can create the culture you'll need to transform results."

Grace appreciated Dan's kindness, support, and wisdom. She vowed to herself that her lack of attention to the four *C*'s model would change immediately.

A Sliver of Hope

As Grace drove across town toward Wisdom after spending most of her Saturday morning with Dan, the things he had shared about the four C's model swam through her head. Grace realized again how she had observed the power of the model while working at Northfield yet had inexplicably failed to give the model much credence in her new role thus far.

Though in the beginning of the conversation with Dan she hadn't felt the four C's would help her in Wisdom's particular situation, the more she thought about it, the more she knew ignoring the four C's during her first days as CEO had been a huge mistake.

Perhaps what Grace had enjoyed most about her visit with Dan was the story he told her in the parking lot just as she was leaving. He shared what Northfield had been like when he first arrived and how he had used the model to turn the struggling operation around. Though the problems he had faced in the beginning were different in some ways, they seemed no less daunting. And although she had heard bits and pieces of the story in the past, it was extremely comforting to be reminded that Northfield wasn't always like it was today.

Grace decided the four C's model had seemed like a simple solution, and because of that, it had been easy for her to dismiss and ignore. She reminded herself again how it had proved invaluable for Dan, and now she knew that through his persistence on focusing on each of the C's,

Northfield had set the standard that other health care centers looked to.

Grace also knew it would take time to build up high levels of clarity, consistency, celebration, and charity at Wisdom. *But I only have six months for it to work.* Grace thought before thinking, *I'm not sure how I'm going to pull this off yet but I'm certainly going figure it out.*

Because of the reality of the situation she found herself in, Grace concluded she needed to focus on implementing the four *C*'s quicker than anyone else ever had if she ever hoped to turn Wisdom around in time. The clock was ticking, and she had already wasted ten days. She felt determined to succeed.

***

Sitting down at her desk at Wisdom, Grace found the notes and the drawing she had made of the four *C*'s model in her notebook. Tearing out the sheet of paper and spreading it in front of her on her desk, she felt for the first time in many days a sliver of hope.

Dan always said the four *C*'s model would help any leader have success, regardless of the industry, situation, or circumstance they found themselves in. If there was ever a time to test the validity of that claim, it was now.

Part One

Clarity and Charity

Hope Grows

Early Sunday morning, Grace sat in her home after getting ready for the day. She was staring at the photocopied version she had made of her four *C*'s model diagram and notes. She wanted to be constantly reminded of them everywhere she went.

Though she knew her husband thought she had gone a little mad over this four *C*'s thing, as he called it, it didn't stop her from making a copy for her home, her car, and her work bag. She also neatly secured the original copy to the right-hand corner of her desk in her office.

Unfortunately, it had been another long, sleepless night, and she was feeling tired. This time, however, the cause of her sleeplessness wasn't due to extreme worry and stress but instead was the result of incessant thoughts about how she could implement each of the four *C*'s immediately at her center. She finally had dozed off in the early hours of the morning. When her alarm went off, she felt like she had only slept a minute.

Despite her sleep deprivation, the good news was she had in her mind what she believed would be a great start to what she called Wisdom's four *C*'s implementation plan.

The first *C* to focus on and establish throughout the center was clarity. As she arrived at her office late Sunday morning, she immediately sat down and sent a group text to the remaining four top-level executives on her team, letting them know she'd like to hold a meeting with them first thing Monday morning. She also surprised herself by confidently sharing with them that she had great reason to hope for Wisdom's turnaround and eventual success, even assuring them the center would rise to become a top performer within Wiser Care, Inc.

Grace wondered if she might have overdone it when she didn't get a response from anyone, but she brushed it off. After all, she knew she hadn't done much yet to earn their trust.

Next, Grace decided it would be helpful to write down what she knew so far about each of her executive team members. After all, she knew their performance was crucial to the success of the center, and her relationship with them would play a pivotal role in their execution of the four C's plan. This also seemed like an important first step to begin to improve charity.

This is what she wrote down.

Marshall, COO—young and new to his role as COO. Has worked at the center for only a few months. Appears to be trying but is struggling in the role. Does seem like a hard worker.

Jenn, VP of rehabilitation—has worked at Wisdom for two years, but it hasn't been smooth. Has openly shared she has considered leaving Wisdom because of the instability and poor clinical care. Is blunt and almost rude and wears her emotions on her sleeve. Seems to really know her stuff and appears to be respected by others in the center.

Bruce, CFO—is on his second stint with the center. Worked at Wisdom many years ago but left to work for a nearby competitor. Returned about nine months ago. Has good experience as a CFO. Though cleanup is still needed, there have been good *improvements in the business office's performance metrics since his return. Business office results seem to be the only metrics trending in the right direction currently. Seems organized and methodical.*

Rosie, VP of HR—the veteran in the group. Very self-confident. Has worked at Wisdom for more than twenty years in various positions. Is a wealth of knowledge about anything to do with the center and seems to be well known throughout it. Has been the only dependable and constant leadership person. Seems to have surprising loyalty to Wisdom despite its many challenges.

Grace looked at what she had written about her team, realizing she knew little about each of them, especially outside work. She also noticed she only had a few nice things to say about them, and this was a problem.

There is no way I can replace my entire leadership team and hope to turn things around quickly, she thought as she looked over her list of executive leaders. She realized she would need to find a way to connect with each of them on a much deeper level—especially if she ever hoped to improve charity.

Peering at the names on her list again, Grace had a troubling thought. *Who on this list might be the next one to resign?* She pushed that notion aside, hoping it wouldn't be any of them anytime soon. Though none were perfect, she knew she needed the help and support of each of them to stabilize what felt like a health care center that was slowly crumbling.

* * *

After what felt like a productive afternoon, Grace was eager to head home and get some sleep. She also actually looked forward to the morning when she could visit with her executive team and officially begin to implement her four *C*'s plan.

This should be interesting, she thought, still unsure of what her team might think about her change in attitude and focus as she drove home through the unusually quiet roads on a late Sunday afternoon.

Surprise

As she entered the room, Grace was surprised to find seven people surrounding the conference room table, rather than only the four executives she had invited to the meeting.

Brittany, the director of HR and Rosie's right-hand woman, along with Luke, the facilities director, and Kristina, the director of dietary services, were the unexpected guests.

Though a little perplexed at first, Grace realized it really shouldn't have been a surprise to her that these additional leaders had been invited by others in the room to attend the meeting. If Grace had learned anything during her short time at the center, it was the fact that the executive team never met and rarely functioned as an actual team. Instead, most everything was done in the larger context of the entire leadership team, which included all department directors and supervisors. This was a problem.

Though the broader leadership team was important, Grace knew she first needed her core leaders to function as a cohesive unit. She knew the strength and alignment of her top-level leaders would be paramount to their eventual turnaround and success. She also knew that the way to achieve this level of unity at the top would only come through establishing the four C's.

After a few awkward moments, Grace politely dismissed the three leaders she had not intended to join the meeting.

As soon as the door closed behind them, Rosie spoke up first. "I'm so sorry for inviting Brittany and Kristina. I just thought your text message meant you wanted all the leaders to attend. I thought we were holding a leadership meeting."

"Me too," chimed in Marshall. "Luke was in my office early this morning, trying to figure out why it's so cold in there. I asked him if he was going to the meeting and told him about it. I didn't think it would be a big deal to have some of our other experienced leaders here with us."

"It's OK," Grace said sincerely. "I certainly could have been clearer in my communication with you about this meeting." After a moment, she added, "As funny as this sounds, this is actually a great introduction to what I want to talk about today. Creating more clarity at Wisdom is something that's been on my mind a lot lately, and it's where I'd like to begin our meeting this morning."

Grace noticed what she thought was a combination of confused and surprised looks around the table. Though the meeting had not started out how she had envisioned it, she knew she had everyone's attention.

Grace then began by introducing the four C's model to her team of executives. She drew the pyramid with each of the C's on their corresponding levels in it and then at the end added a big circle around it and explained what charity was and how it worked in the model. She then shared how she believed if they all committed to establishing each of the C's firmly at their center, it would completely turn around their struggling operation.

Grace noticed most in the room seemed only mildly impressed by what she had just shared, but this didn't bother her. Based on the current situation, how she had behaved to that point, and the problems the center had been facing for a long while, she knew it probably felt like a big stretch to believe that this model would really help. In fact,

Grace had had her own doubts even after having experienced the power of the model firsthand while working at Northfield. She knew at first glance it probably appeared too simplistic and even theoretical. How could a few leadership principles that were so obvious help them overcome their complex problems?

"By only looking at the model, it can sometimes be hard to detect the true power that lies within the fundamental tenets contained in it," Grace now said. "But when these four elements of the model are well established together, it creates an incredible organizational culture and transforms results. This model and its leadership principles are the secret to Northfield's success. They can also become our secret to success here at Wisdom."

Grace knew her executives were well acquainted with Northfield. Not only were Northfield's results legendary throughout the company, but the fact that Wisdom was only a short thirty-five-minute drive across town made them that much more known by this particular group of leaders.

Without any open objections from her team at this point, Grace knew it was time to shift the conversation and introduce where they were going to begin with their four C's implementation plan.

Building Blocks

"Based on the model, our first step to improving our culture and our performance is to establish clarity. And I think a good place to start would be with clarifying the roles and responsibilities of this team," Grace said, noticing a few surprised looks.

"It's my understanding this group has not been functioning as a true executive team. Am I right?"

A few around the table nodded, and Grace went on.

"From what I've gathered, this team hasn't been meeting regularly or collaborating on important decisions in the center—at least not as much as I'd like to see. Based on my observations, most decisions are made in isolation, normally by the CEO, and then simply communicated to others."

Though it appeared that there might have been a rebuttal coming from Bruce, he didn't actually say anything, so after a moment, Grace decided to continue.

"From now on, the leaders most critical to our health care center's success will make up our executive leadership team. This includes everyone in this room, as well as the new VP of clinical services and the new VP of marketing, once we fill these open positions. And hopefully we can fill them soon, so we have a complete and fully functioning executive team."

Grace paused for a moment and then added, "I'd like this team to meet weekly, and I'd like to propose Monday mornings around this same time. Is everyone OK with that?"

After a short discussion, the group settled on midmorning every Monday. This would allow time to check on things from the weekend before gathering.

Grace then said, "This executive team will be the primary decision-making body within our health care center. We will hash out what we need to do collectively to improve results with a focus on establishing the C's contained in the model. And each of us will be held responsible for all the results within the center and not just our individual responsibilities."

Grace let that sink in for a moment until Bruce said, "Does this mean our weekly leadership meeting will go away then?"

"No," Grace quickly responded. "Our broader leadership team will continue to function as is, and we will continue to hold our weekly leadership team meeting, which includes all the department heads and directors throughout the center.

"Our executive team, however, will be a subset of this broader leadership team and, as I mentioned before, will consist of those leaders who have the greatest ability and responsibility to influence the outcomes within our health care center—or, in other words, us. Our weekly executive team meeting will not replace our weekly leadership team meeting but will be in addition to it."

"Oh great, more meetings," Marshall said sarcastically, as if attempting to make a joke. A few smiled, mostly out of pity for the ill-timed comment.

Grace then shared more about why the executive team was important, how they would function, and what the plan would be for their meeting each week. After establishing a certain level of clarity about the role, function, and importance of the executive team, Grace wanted to bring up the topic she had intended to be the main focus of the meeting in the first place.

"Now that we've talked about the makeup and dynamics of our executive team, I'd like to talk more about how we can create clarity at our center and, specifically, clarity around the building blocks of a strong organization. These building blocks will set the foundation for our culture. Everything we do from here on out will be built on them.

"Does everyone know what these building blocks are?"

Grace noticed most looking away and avoiding eye contact. She knew immediately it was an unfair question. The truth was Grace had learned so much from Dan about the four C's model she often forgot not everyone had had the opportunity to work with him and learn from him.

She quickly responded to her own question. "The building blocks of a strong organization are the company's mission, vision, and core values." Grace noticed a few relaxing as she shared the answer.

"So we're going to start here with clarifying these three most important items. These three items are the basis for meaningful work, and for this reason, this is where organizational clarity must begin. Until we're clear about what our mission, vision, and values are, we won't make lasting progress here. And this understanding needs to start with us—this core group of leaders. We must know each of these three building blocks inside and out, and then we must commit to living by them."

Grace wondered what her team might be thinking at this point. It was hard to tell. She decided to press on.

"Can anyone tell me what our current mission statement, vision, and core values are here at Wisdom?"

Grace observed most in the room were now looking like deer caught in headlights. It was evident again that they were unsure. She reasoned they probably hadn't heard much talk about a mission, vision, or values for a long time, but she didn't want to let them off the hook without giving them some time.

After another moment, Bruce finally spoke up, and that encouraged some of the other leaders in the room to try as well. None were able to properly state the current mission statement, and together they were only able to identify a few of the core values.

Grace finally decided to rescue them from their feeble attempts. "Currently, the mission for our health care center is long and too hard to remember or understand. I really don't blame anyone for not knowing it. It would probably take me months of practice to memorize that thing." She noticed a few relax as she reassured them it was OK.

"I think it would help us make things clearer if we cut back the mission statement to one easy-to-understand and easy-to-digest sentence that gives each person who works here a clear purpose. Without a clear, shared, unifying purpose that we are all striving for each day, it will be hard to pull ourselves out of all the troubles we currently find ourselves in here."

Grace detected some reservation. She wondered if she should say something about it but decided it could wait. She then continued, "We need to be coming to work with a clear purpose—all of us. The question we need to answer with our mission statement is 'What are we trying to accomplish day in and day out here at Wisdom?' Or what is the point of our daily efforts?"

Grace could still feel hesitancy from the group, but she wanted them to understand how important a clear and concise mission statement would be for their health care center. She knew she needed a different approach.

"Imagine for a moment that everyone on our team was truly working toward the same purpose each day. Imagine if you walked down our halls and asked any team member their purpose at work, they all responded with the same answer. Imagine if each and every last person who worked here truly felt a higher purpose for their job, more than just to complete a task or collect a paycheck."

Grace could tell the leaders in the room were now contemplating what she was sharing, so she waited another moment and then pushed on. "For example, what if, instead of believing they were simply mopping a floor each day, our housekeepers believed they were saving lives because in many ways they are, through controlling the spread of infection.

"Or if our cooks believed that, rather than just preparing food, they were creating a memorable event. Or if our nurses were focused on creating great experiences for their patients rather than simply administering a medication or treatment. How might things be different here at Wisdom if this was the case for our team members? If each worked with a clear purpose in mind?"

Grace leaned back now, hoping her team would open up.

Finally, it was Bruce who broke the silence again. "I think it would change people's attitudes. Too many of our staff don't recognize the important work they are engaged in here. In health care, you would think this would be obvious."

"Good point, Bruce. And I think that's one reason why we don't talk about our purpose enough—because we assume everyone already knows how important the work we do here is . . . Any other thoughts?"

"It would probably make a big difference in how people felt about working here too," Rosie added.

"And it would help us feel like we're more of a team. Too many people don't recognize how what they do affects others around them, and too many of our people act as if they aren't in this together," Marshall now chimed in.

"It would totally change people's perspective about work," Jenn said, sounding almost enthusiastic. She then added, "And it would absolutely improve our quality of care."

"And all our results," Rosie now commented.

Grace was both relieved and excited by the answers. She felt her team was slowly starting to catch the vision of how effective what she was sharing could truly be. She waited another moment to make sure there wasn't anything else anyone wanted to add. She then said, "I think all of you are right. If each person who works for Wisdom understands, believes in, and works toward the same purpose, or our mission, day in and day out, that alone could have a significant impact on our results. This is what having a shared purpose or mission can do for our center. It will align us around a common cause. It will make it clear we are all on the same team. Establishing a mission that we live by will have a tangible effect on all our results."

The few leaders in the room were slowly nodding before Rosie said, "But we've already had a mission statement, and it hasn't seemed to help too much."

"Good point," Grace said. "It's not helping. Any ideas on why that might be?"

"Because there is a lack of clarity," Jenn said matter-of-factly. "First, our mission statement itself is not very clear, and second, we've done little to make sure it is well known. I mean, we rarely refer to it, and just a minute ago, none of us could even share what it was."

"Exactly," Grace said, thrilled by Jenn's response. "But all this is going to change starting today."

She then paused a moment to let what they had discussed sink in before adding, "And it's not just our purpose that's unclear. From my perspective, nobody knows where we're headed and what we hope to ultimately accomplish. So we could be going anywhere, and it wouldn't really matter because we don't have a known, desired destination for all our efforts. Would anyone disagree that we lack a clear sense of direction or vision?"

The other executives in the room were slowly shaking their heads, and Jenn even offered an audible, "No, not really."

"In a way, this means our team could take any road they wish because our destination is inconsequential, or at least it seems that way because we haven't made it clear."

"But if we had a clear direction or vision, then our people would take more actions that would move us toward that destination? Is that what you're saying?" Marshall offered.

"Exactly!" Grace said, impressed with her young COO's comment. "Just like with our mission, a clear vision will unify us and help us remember where we want to eventually end up. Having a clearly defined long-term objective will again align our team and provide similar benefits that having a clear mission will provide to our team."

"I like that idea of deciding where we are going," Rosie commented.

"Me too," added Jenn.

"The final building block is our core values, and it seems like, just as with the other two, no one around here knows them well, or if they do, they don't understand them, and they don't try to live by them. And it's a big problem if our top executives don't even know them."

Grace noticed one leader in the room look down and another look away.

"I don't blame you for not knowing them at this moment. Before today, I'm not sure they were ever important or relevant, but soon, this group will need to not only know them but also set the example of living them."

Grace stood quickly and walked over to the whiteboard where she had drawn the basic diagram of the four C's model earlier. She added the three building blocks below the clarity section and returned to her seat at the table.

"Our team here in this room needs to come up with a clear and concise mission statement, well-defined core values, and a vision that is inspiring. These three vital building blocks will set the stage not only for clarity within our health care center but also for our eventual turnaround and success. They will provide meaning for work and be the foundation of our culture here at Wisdom. Thoughts?"

Grace now tried to sit back and relax as she looked around the room at the other leaders, who were beginning to look at one another. Finally, Rosie asked, "Are you saying we need to throw out our current mission statement and core values altogether?"

Grace hesitated for just a second, unsure of what her team thought about that idea, especially Rosie, who had been working at the center for so long, before answering, "Yes. We need to develop an updated mission statement, core values, and vision for our center that will provide clarity around our purpose, what we stand for and believe in, and where we're headed. This doesn't mean we have to throw everything out, though. If there is anything we'd like to incorporate that will help us define our purpose, direction, and beliefs, then we should. We just need to make sure what we come up with is clear, easy to understand, and inspiring."

Grace noticed Rosie seemed fine with what she had said when Jenn commented with some enthusiasm, "This all sounds great."

"And each building block must be something each of us in this room is excited about. Because we all must get behind them one hundred percent. They will become our common, shared, unified cause."

It appeared everyone in the room was feeling good about what she had just shared except Bruce, who looked stoic and was hard to read. Grace decided it was time to ask him for his thoughts.

"What do you think about this, Bruce?"

After some hesitation, Bruce said, "I don't know about all this, truthfully. It sounds nice but also very utopian. I'm sorry to be so frank here, but honestly, every company I've worked for before has had a mission statement and some values, and it never seems to matter much. I'm just not sure this should be our highest priority right now. I mean, have you seen our numbers lately? We're struggling to even survive."

Grace understood where Bruce was coming from. Though she disagreed with his perspective, she appreciated his honest concern.

"Thank you, Bruce, for being open and for pushing back on this idea. We need more of that as we make important decisions together and move forward. This team needs to be able to call each other out and question each other. It will no longer be OK to sit back and become a spectator as things continue to decline here."

Grace noticed that all eyes were riveted on her, and she could tell everyone was wondering what she might say next. Rather than being the only voice on the subject, she decided to get others involved.

"So what does everyone think about Bruce's worries?"

Jenn didn't hesitate and jumped in. "If these things aren't made clear, Bruce, I don't think we'll ever get to a point where we aren't struggling to survive. It will just continue to be a fragmented team and continual chaos."

"I agree with Jenn. Most people want to work for a cause nowadays. They aren't satisfied or motivated with just a paycheck anymore," Marshall added.

"No thanks to your generation," Bruce said with a quick smile, and everyone laughed.

Marshall then commented, "And without a clear identity for our health care center that a defined purpose, values, and vision can provide, it's going to be difficult for us to build a team and recruit others to join us. We'll just be like any other employer out there who offers people a meaningless job and a paycheck."

Rosie seemed to perk up with Marshall's comment, adding, "I agree completely. And by all indications, what we have been doing previously hasn't been working."

"I agree we can't continue to do the same old things, and our team is clearly fragmented, no matter how hard we've tried to pull them together," Bruce now said, appearing to be thinking through his thoughts and finally adding, "but do we really think this will do the trick? I'm not sure how this makes us different from others."

Though his questions weren't directed specifically to her, Grace decided it was time to jump in. "I understand your hesitancy, Bruce. Having these building blocks alone won't necessarily make us different. But operationalizing them through the four C's model will make us different. If we can make them alive through clarity, consistency, and celebration, it will shape and improve everything we do here."

Grace hesitated, noticing that Bruce still seemed unsure. "I've come from a health care center that was in a situation similar to what we find ourselves in, and the leaders over there applied this model starting with the building blocks. This was the first step they took and the most important. They've now become the top center in our entire company. If nothing else, it's hard to question those results."

Grace wasn't sure what Bruce was thinking at this point, but after a moment, he said, "No one can question Northfield's results; they've been a beacon of excellence in the industry for years. If we could even become half of what they are today, it would be phenomenal."

Everyone in the room was now nodding their heads.

"If you're that confident this is where we need to focus our energies at this time, then I will trust you. And honestly, I haven't been able to come up with any better plan yet," Bruce said with a slight grin.

Grace was grateful Bruce had shared his honest thoughts without reservation and was also pleased with his willingness to put his personal opinions aside and trust the rest of the team.

"Thank you. I appreciate your trust and support more than you know," Grace said sincerely. She looked around the room and saw a level of excitement on the faces of her colleagues that she hadn't seen before. She sensed they all were genuinely interested in what they had been tasked with doing—clarifying the building blocks for Wisdom Health Care Center.

Creating Clarity

Before the executive team dove in, Grace described in further detail what each of the three individual building blocks should clarify. She explained that the mission should answer the question of why each team member came to work each day, or what their purpose was day in and day out.

Then she shared how the vision should answer where they were headed and the eventual contribution they hoped one day to make to the world.

Next, she explained how the core values should answer how they would strive to behave and act to help them live their mission and achieve their vision. Their values would establish the specific standards and guidelines that were most important to the center.

Finally, she reiterated how the building blocks provided clarity around the most important questions people wanted to know, whether consciously or not.

She also described how they worked together—how living the core values would help them accomplish their mission each day and how living their mission and values day in and day out would then allow them to achieve their vision.

With what felt like palpable energy in the room, the team brainstormed a few ideas about each of the building blocks and looked at what might be of some value from their current mission and values. After some further discussion and debate, Grace realized how late it was in the day.

"I think we've made some great progress here, and I'm confident that creating these building blocks will alter the current trajectory of Wisdom. I'm also convinced there is nothing more important than to begin to create clarity throughout our center, especially around these building blocks.

"Let's end our meeting and take some time individually to think more about what we've discussed today and come back together with our ideas."

Though the meeting had lasted much longer than expected, Grace felt it had been some of the most productive time she had spent thus far as a CEO.

Before everyone left the conference room, the team of executives agreed to meet again Wednesday afternoon to attempt to solidify the building blocks for their health care center.

Showing Charity

Though the meeting had gone long, Grace knew there was something else she needed to start before the day ended. Understanding clarity was the base of the model and the first step to establishing a strong culture, she also knew charity was an element of the model that needed attention throughout the entire process.

"The higher the levels of charity in an organization, the bigger the impact the efforts in establishing the other three *C*'s have on the culture," Dan would always say whenever he spoke about the model. And working at Northfield, she had witnessed this firsthand.

Additionally, Grace wondered if she might always be haunted by that moment when Dan had questioned her about showing charity to her new team. The memory stung but served as an important wake-up call.

Still feeling a little unsure about how she could effectively elevate charity levels, she remembered what Dan had said—that one of the best ways to show someone at work you care about them is by getting to know them better.

With this piece of advice cemented in her brain, Grace came up with three simple ideas on how she could begin to raise the levels of charity immediately. This is what she wrote down.

```
                My Charity-Building Tasks

    1.  Do daily rounds with the main objective being to
        get to know my team. At a minimum, I will:
        a.   Walk the floors of the center each
             morning first thing when I arrive at
             work.
        b.   Walk the floors each evening before I
             leave work.
    2.  Write at least one personalized thank-you note
        to a team member each day.
    3.  Get to know the names of as many employees as
        possible.
```

The first item on her list was to begin to do rounds
throughout her health care center. In other words, she
would walk the floor of the center at least twice each day
and spend time with her team in their work areas. Though
she believed walking the halls would give her some
valuable insight into the operation of the center, her number
one priority during these daily rounds was to get to know
her team and build rapport with them.

Grace believed if the staff truly got to know her,
they'd see she was genuinely interested in them and the
team's success. She thought this simple practice of walking
the floors each morning and evening would be a great way
to increase charity levels. She soon found she was right.

* * *

During her first official round, Grace met several staff
members she had seen a few times before but had never
taken the time to get to know. While many she spoke with
were contracted employees, one nurse who caught her
attention happened to be employed by the center.

Grace discovered that her name was Kaylee and that she was a long-tenured team member by Wisdom's standards, as she had been working there for nearly five years. Grace thought she looked exhausted. As their conversation continued, she soon learned why.

"This is my second double shift in the last four days. I've probably averaged working over seventy hours the last few weeks, and honestly, I'm tired," Kaylee said.

Grace learned from Kaylee that because there were so many open positions, many were being asked to work a lot of extra shifts. Grace thanked Kaylee for her sacrifices and efforts to care for their patients and reassured her that improving staffing was one of her top priorities.

After some more chitchat, Kaylee opened up more and confessed she was constantly wondering if she should look for work elsewhere. She had seen many of her coworkers come and go at the center, and she often questioned why she wasn't following suit. She disclosed that she was one of only a small contingent of loyal staff members on her unit trying to stick it out during these hard times but that it wasn't easy, and the team often talked openly about working elsewhere. Finally, she shared that she was hopeful things would improve soon with Grace starting.

Hearing this, Grace was immediately unnerved about the idea of losing more staff, and she knew she didn't want to lose Kaylee or any of the other remaining team members for that matter. She wasn't sure what she could do for her in the moment, but she sincerely thanked her again for her openness and reassured her things were going to get better soon.

As Grace returned to her office, she had mixed emotions. First, she felt dejected all over again by the staffing crisis she was facing at her center. After gaining more perspective into how it was affecting her team, she felt an increased level of urgency to improve it.

On the other hand, she felt surprised by the people she had met and their dedication to work. Many of them seemed capable, caring, and willing to work hard. In a way, her perception of her team had already changed. She also felt better because of the relationships she was beginning to form with some of them.

Like her meeting in the morning, her first round had taken much longer than she had anticipated, but also like her meeting, she believed it had been a success and time well spent.

As she sat back down behind her desk, she decided it was time to do the second task on her list to grow charity.

Grace knew exactly who she needed to write her first thank-you note to.

A Note

At the end of Kaylee's shift, Grace handed her the thank-you note she had written and expressed again her sincere appreciation for all she was doing. Grace felt good about offering this small gesture of appreciation and couldn't help but notice the look of surprise on Kaylee's face as she took the card. Grace hoped if nothing else, Kaylee would at least feel she had been heard and was appreciated.

As she sat back down in her office, she looked at the final task on her short charity building list, which read "Get to know the names of as many employees as possible." She then thought about the team members she had gotten to know earlier that day and realized she had forgotten the names of many of them. She vowed to do better on her next round.

* * *

As Grace prepared to head out the door late that evening, she remembered she hadn't done her second round. Though she was tired and desperately wanted to go home, she changed direction and began to walk the halls of her center.

Unlike her round earlier in the day, this time she began making a list of the names of staff members she met. She even asked a few for permission to snap their picture with her cell phone and added them as contacts. Many seemed flattered by this, although one or two seemed puzzled by her actions. Regardless, she knew it would help.

Though her husband would undoubtedly think she was acting a little crazy again, Grace planned to study their names and faces before her evening round tomorrow. Her goal was to be able to come back the next day and say hello, calling as many of her team members by name as she possibly could. Though this felt like a small act in the grand scheme of things, she was certain it was another way to increase charity levels in the center.

As Grace headed home that night later than she expected, she felt a sense of connectedness to the center she hadn't experienced before. She realized she now knew some of the people inside its walls on a more personal level, and this brought more feelings of attachment and responsibility toward them. She knew this was a good thing.

Though it had been another challenging day, this time, Grace believed she had made real progress toward improving things at Wisdom. She felt a surprising sense of satisfaction that she hadn't had during her previous trips home. She was certain it was because of her focus on the four *C*'s model.

Ad Hoc Executive Meeting

It was now Wednesday afternoon, and Grace found herself surrounded by her executive team once again in the conference room. However, things felt different than when they first met Monday morning. The energy in the room was higher, and her team seemed more enthusiastic to be there.

As the meeting progressed, Grace was thrilled by what her team was sharing and discussing with one another. The ideas that were brought to the table were good, and everyone seemed fully invested in creating the right building blocks that would move the health care center forward. Grace noticed that the opportunity to shape the direction and culture of the health care center sparked a renewed sense of passion she hadn't otherwise seen in many of her top leaders.

Grace made it a point to emphasize throughout the process that they were shaping not only the culture but also the trajectory of Wisdom. She reminded them that their work today would be remembered for a long time.

After some good debates and multiple revisions, the team had developed a final mission statement, core values, and a vision for their center. Grace wrote them on the whiteboard.

MISSION
Wisdom Health Care Center's mission is to provide an exceptional experience for each person it serves.

CORE VALUES

Wisdom Health Care Center's Core values are:

Employee Dedicated

- We are devoted to creating a culture of fulfillment for all our team members.
- We seek to provide excellent work opportunities in an environment that encourages team members to thrive and take pride in the service they deliver.
- We believe being "employee dedicated" translates into the best customer care and the greatest results.

Ownership

- We take ownership of our conduct, behavior, attitudes, and actions.
- We take ownership of our mistakes and always strive to improve.
- We act like owners in all that we do, and we understand the responsibility and trust we have been given.
- We take ownership of our results and never make excuses.

Customer Care

- We look for opportunities to delight our customers.
- We define our customers as anyone who enters our center, including patients, family members, physicians, vendors, coworkers, and our community.

- We strive to "wow" our customers through creating special experiences and lasting memories.

Greatness
- We define greatness as doing our best every day and helping others do the same.
- We hold ourselves to the highest standards of conduct and professionalism.
- We do not settle for simply good, because we know we have the capacity to be great.
- We believe everyone has the ability to be great every single day.

VISION
Wisdom Health Care Center's vision is to have a lasting impact on the industry by becoming a health care center others look to, learn from, and aspire to become.

Grace couldn't have been more excited about what they had come up with and how clearly they had defined the building blocks of their health care center. She could tell others on her leadership team were happy about them too.

Grace felt the first steps of laying the foundation toward creating clarity throughout the center had been taken. She recognized, however, that they still had a long road ahead of them to make the building blocks clear to everyone.

After they had been together for the entirety of the afternoon ironing out the building blocks, the executive team decided to take a break. Yet each readily agreed to reconvene in two hours and work into the evening to come up with an initial plan to effectively share the new mission, vision, and values with others.

* * *

During their evening meeting, the team talked about how they could introduce and reinforce the new building blocks to create clarity throughout the entire organization. Being unapologetically old school, Grace wrote down their plan on her notepad. This is what it looked like.

Wisdom HC's Building Blocks Clarity Plan

1. Hold a leadership team meeting with all company leaders, department heads, and supervisors tomorrow at 10:00 a.m. to introduce the mission, vision, and values.
2. Present the mission, vision, and values at the next all-staff meeting, scheduled for next Tuesday.
3. Create a one-page document with the mission, vision, and values and distribute it to each team member at the all-staff meeting.
4. Update the employee handbook to reflect the changes to the mission, vision, and values.
5. Hang a copy of the mission, vision, and values in each executive team member's office and in the leadership conference room.
6. Share and discuss the mission, vision, and values as an agenda item in each leadership meeting moving forward.

Though they had left the meeting certain they would eventually need to add more items to their plan, all agreed it felt like a good start.

As each executive team member left the conference room, Grace detected hope in their eyes. Hope was something she had noticed was lacking at Wisdom, and she believed many of the staff hadn't felt much hope there for a long time. She desperately wanted to restore a sense of hope throughout the entire center and knew they had taken an important first step.

Surprising Call

Though the last few days had continued to be challenging, things felt better as Grace practiced what she now was calling her "charity habits." These included daily rounds with the primary purpose of getting to know her team, writing a daily thank-you note to a deserving team member, and learning as many of her employees' names as possible. She now decided to add one more item to her list.

Early that morning, Grace had asked Rosie for a list of all employee birthdays. She recalled receiving personal birthday cards from Dan each year and remembered how meaningful they were to her. She suspected one reason she valued them so much was that she knew how busy he was. Despite the many demands on his time, the annual birthday card communicated to her that he knew her, was interested in her, and cared enough to recognize her on her birthday. She saw it as an action that had raised charity at Northfield and now wanted to do the same at Wisdom. Writing a personal birthday card to each team member became the fourth charity habit on her growing list.

While writing her first few birthday cards, Grace felt her phone vibrate in her pocket. She saw it was Tom and quickly answered the call.

"Hello, Tom."

"Hi, Grace, how are you? How's the center?" Tom asked.

"Well, I can tell you I've felt inadequate and overwhelmed, but I believe we are starting to make progress."

Tom then said something that seemed uncharacteristic of him and completely caught Grace by surprise. "What kind of progress are you talking about, Grace?"

Before she could respond, Tom went on.

"Listen, I'm calling because I've seen no change in patient volume over there since you started. In fact, if anything, it has declined slightly. It also looks as if our daily staffing expenses haven't changed all that much either.

"You understand this will give us the same results we've always had over there, right? We need to see changes and improvements now."

Grace felt a moment of panic, followed by a surge of anger. It had been less than three weeks since her first day at the center, and she had spent nearly every waking hour trying to stabilize the operation. It had practically been a war zone when she had arrived. She hadn't heard a peep from Tom during those first weeks.

This is the first thing he calls to tell me, she thought. Grace felt like letting Tom have it, but she kept her cool.

"Thanks, Tom, for watching out for us. I think we really are finally making progress, though it may not be reflected in the numbers yet. I've looked closely at staffing, and we'll be making some changes soon, but I believe our approach to this is important. We want to establish some consistency around how we do things here. I also feel confident our patient volume will grow soon with the changes that are taking place."

"I hope you're right, Grace. You know the pressure and timeline we're under at Wisdom. I had hoped for more progress by now. I know it hasn't been long; it's just . . ." Tom hesitated for a minute before adding, "We may have even less time than I thought." Tom was silent for a moment before adding, "I'm sorry. I know you can do it. Please keep me posted."

Tom ended the call abruptly before Grace was able to get good answers about the new timeline for the possible sale of the center. She put down her phone, feeling both a little nervous and incredibly disheartened. *Less time? But it takes time for the four C's to take hold and have an impact.*

Grace worried she might not have enough time to reap the full benefits of her efforts around establishing each of the *C*'s throughout the health care center. She knew she needed to speed up the process and do more right away. *How can I accelerate the implementation of the four C's?*

Though she anticipated it might not be well received by her team, she had an idea of just how to do it.

Daily Huddle

"Another meeting," Marshall said, trying to sound sarcastic but failing once again with his poorly timed joke.

"I know it sounds like I'm asking a lot, but I can assure you it will pay off," Grace explained to her executive team. She could tell there was a lot of skepticism surrounding the idea she had just presented to them.

"So Dan did this at Northfield?" Bruce asked, sounding incredulous. "And every day?"

"Yes," Grace answered. "We had a great system in place at Northfield. Not only did it help us create clarity, but it also helped with establishing most of the other C's in the model as well. Meeting as a leadership team each day sounds like a big deal right now, but it won't be once we get in the habit of doing it. This daily meeting will give us the opportunity to iron out any dangling details, quickly resolve issues, ensure we are all on the same page, and align our focus and efforts on the most important things."

"And you believe this will help us save time?" This time it was Rosie. She sounded sincere rather than skeptical about what her CEO had just introduced. Grace believed she might be warming up to the idea.

"That's right. Remember, this daily huddle is meant to be a ten-minute meeting where we quickly share our priorities for the day and ask any questions we need answers to from others on our team."

"And how does that help us save time?" It was Bruce again. Though feeling a little annoyed at this point, Grace knew it was a legitimate question. Her team deserved to understand how this daily meeting would help them.

She thought for a moment until she remembered a recent example. "Remember a few days ago when we were trying to resolve the insurance questions Ms. Johnson brought up when her mother was admitted late in the evening?"

"How could anyone forget that?" Marshall said emphatically.

Grace pushed on. "Since they arrived after normal hours, our nursing team couldn't get her an answer right away, which frustrated her, and she soon became very upset. Our nurses then called the evening supervisor, who assured Ms. Johnson that she'd have an answer in the morning."

Most in the room were nodding.

"The evening supervisor then sent an email to the social services director about Ms. Johnson's concerns. Once the social services director saw the message the next morning, she emailed you, right, Bruce? Asking if you knew about her insurance?" Grace said this as more of a statement then a question. "And then you weren't sure about the specifics, so you went to the business office manager, who then reached out to the nursing supervisor for clarification about what specifically Ms. Johnson wanted to know about her mother's insurance."

"And unfortunately, the nursing supervisor was tied up," Bruce now said.

"That's right, and before long, it was noon, and no one had followed up with Ms. Johnson. We sort of dropped the ball—at least in her mind, we did.

"Then, by early afternoon, Marshall was getting an earful from Ms. Johnson about something he knew nothing about. He was completely confused about why she was so upset and yelling at him."

"That is true. My ear is still sore from that tongue lashing I received," Marshall said, rubbing his ear with a slight smile.

"Then Marshall ran to your office, Bruce, to try and get information about the insurance for Ms. Johnson. You then both called the business office manager, who was then able to make a few more phone calls to the nurse supervisor and social services director before nailing down the exact information Ms. Johnson was seeking. The business office manager then relayed the information to the social services director, who tried to get in touch with Ms. Johnson, but by this time, it was 5 p.m., and Ms. Johnson was now shouting at my assistant, demanding to speak to the person in charge of this place immediately."

Grace paused to take a breath before adding, "I think I have all my facts straight on this one, but please correct me if I'm wrong."

"You may have missed a few back-and-forths in there," Bruce said with a bit of a smile.

Grace smiled back and then said, "Now imagine we are having a daily huddle each morning for a few minutes, and the social services director shares the message she received from the night supervisor about Ms. Johnson's concern. With all the pertinent leaders together in the same room, we could have had a quick discussion about it and decided who would take responsibility for getting Ms. Johnson an answer as soon as possible. With a daily huddle, we probably could have ironed this out in less than two minutes and saved face with Ms. Johnson."

"And my ear wouldn't be so sore," Marshall quipped.

"Not only would it have saved us time, but in this case, it would have improved our ability to serve our customers and live our mission," Grace added.

Jenn had been unusually quiet for most of the meeting, but she finally said, "Let's be honest. This kind of stuff happens all the time here."

Grace had noticed Jenn appeared to be the most open to the idea from the beginning. She was glad she had pointed this out.

"That's true," Rosie agreed, adding, "and our social services director, our business office manager, our nursing supervisor, Marshall, and you"—she motioned toward Bruce—"all would have been present in this quick morning huddle. So you all would have been on the same page."

"Something that had a relatively easy solution took all day and distracted many of you from your work," Grace added.

"Just imagine the amount of time you would have saved by attending a ten- to fifteen-minute morning huddle," Jenn said to Bruce with a sarcastic smile.

Bruce laughed out loud and shrugged his shoulders as if he couldn't deny it.

Grace looked around the room, unsure if everyone was on board with the idea or not.

"I think I like this idea of a daily morning huddle," Marshall finally offered, breaking the moment of silence.

"I'm thinking about another situation," Rosie now said. "Last Thursday, we had that new employee show up to work, and she couldn't remember who she was supposed to meet with or where she was supposed to go. Somehow, she wasn't greeted by our receptionist in the front lobby, and she apparently wandered around the halls trying to figure out where she needed to be. She eventually found herself in the dietary manager's office, and they told her new employees always start on Monday and that she must have come in on the wrong day."

"Of course, since that was our normal practice until a few weeks ago," Bruce said.

"Exactly. If we held a daily morning huddle, every leader would be aware that new nursing staff are starting as soon as possible now. So it might be on any day of the week." Rosie added.

"And if we quickly mention who is starting that day in the morning meeting, all leaders could at least be aware that a new person is coming. Then, if they're spotted, we'd at least have an idea of who they were and where we could direct them," Jenn said.

"We might even consider giving them a warm welcome if we see them," Marshall chimed in with a wink and a smile.

"Did you hear what happened?" Rosie asked.

"What happened to what?" Marshall responded, looking confused.

"That new employee didn't show up the next day and hasn't returned since. Evidently, our poor communication turned her off."

"That's horrible," Bruce now said.

Grace felt frustrated listening to what had transpired. It was a reminder of how far the center needed to go to improve clarity.

Rosie's story did serve its purpose, though, as it seemed to erase any remaining doubts about the need for a quick morning huddle. Grace was at least grateful for that.

"I think I'm not out of line by saying we all agree a quick daily morning huddle with our entire leadership team might be valuable for us in improving clarity, am I right?" Everyone around the table nodded.

"Remember, it will take us a few days to get used to the process of the meeting, so it may take us a little extra time in the beginning. However, once we get in the habit of having this meeting, it should take us no more than ten minutes to all get on the same page."

Grace noticed that most were again nodding.

"It's important we don't forget that the main objective of the meeting is to provide clarity and align our entire leadership team on the critical priorities each day. And trust me, as we get good at this, it will save us a lot of time and headaches."

"It will also give us a chance to rub shoulders each day and look into each other's eyeballs. I think that's important," Rosie added.

"Yes, I miss seeing Bruce when he hides away in his office for days." Though it seemed Marshall was trying to be funny again, Bruce looked up and gave him a cold stare that silenced the room. Grace noticed Marshall's cheeks turning red when Bruce suddenly laughed out loud.

Everyone in the room began to laugh as well recognizing Bruce wasn't upset and had been teasing Marshall.

After some more ribbing among the group, Grace decided everyone was satisfied with the decision. They then selected a time and location for the daily morning huddle and determined how they would communicate the new meeting to each member of the leadership team who was to attend.

Grace concluded by stating, "Soon we won't be able to imagine our lives without it."

Early Morning Surprise

As Grace pulled into the parking lot at Wisdom at 4:30 a.m., she asked herself why she had decided to come to work so early. It had been a long night the day before and she hadn't wanted to get out of bed, but here she was.

As she walked through the door, she instantly noticed how much quieter the health care center seemed at this hour. She quickly went to her office, grabbed the birthday card she had written out the day before, and began to do her morning round on the floor.

After spending some time checking on things and walking the floor, she finally saw the employee she was looking for. "Happy Birthday, Tamara!" Grace said as enthusiastically as she possibly could that early in the morning.

Grace had only met Tamara once before. And as fate would have it, as soon as she had added handing out personalized birthday cards to all the Wisdom team members as a charity habit, a third-shift certified nursing assistant, Tamara, was having a birthday.

"I wanted to make sure I caught you on your birthday before your shift ended," Grace added with a smile.

Tamara first looked at Grace and seemed confused, almost as if she didn't know who she was, but then suddenly, the expression on her face turned to surprise.

"This is for me?" she asked, reaching out and taking hold of the card with one hand while throwing her other arm around Grace.

"Yup, and thank you for working on your birthday. I hope you take some time to celebrate today."

Tamara stepped back, looking at Grace. "I'm not sure a CEO has ever known my name, let alone when my birthday was. This is truly a shock."

Tamara was shaking her head as if in disbelief. Grace felt a little embarrassed, unsure of what to say, but added, "I really appreciate you working this shift. I know it's not easy."

After another moment Tamara finally said, "Thank you," and Grace noticed tears were forming at the corners of her eyes.

"No problem," Grace responded, and with that, Tamara turned around, wiped her eyes, and headed for a patient room that had a call light lit down the hall.

Wow, that was pretty incredible, Grace thought, and any regret she had had for waking up so early had completely washed away.

Not Satisfied

It was now Friday, and her first three and a half weeks at Wisdom had been a whirlwind. Though it had been a really rough start, Grace did feel they were finally making progress, although the financial performance didn't show it.

As much as it disgusted her, what Tom had shared with her a few days ago was right. The financial results at Wisdom for the month looked similar to the way it had been nearly every month for the last few years.

Grace was now looking at the center's net income graph. This is what it looked like.

Though this month's results weren't much better than the average net income over the previous twelve months, Grace knew things were progressing. For example, earlier in the day, Grace and the team had made an important decision about clinical leadership at the center. With vacancies in the top two leadership roles in the department, an internal team member had been identified as a possible candidate for one of the open positions.

Grace and other leadership team members had interviewed her and watched her closely over the last week. Grace had observed that this individual had proved to be invaluable in stabilizing the department with the sudden departure of the top leaders. Grace and her executive team were impressed and felt she was a great choice as their new director of clinical services.

Now she needed to find a VP of clinical services who could mold, mentor, and support this developing nurse leader. Thankfully, Grace did have a few good leads for this critical role, including a recommendation from the VP of clinical services she had worked alongside at Northfield. This particular candidate seemed the most promising, and Grace was grateful for the recommendation.

In addition to this, after speaking to many physicians, vendors, and other providers in the area, Grace believed she had identified the top VP of marketing in the area. Though she hadn't met him personally, she was determined to meet with him. Thus, she had been persistent in reaching out to him, and after some steady encouragement each time she spoke with him, she was finally able to schedule a meeting with him. After Tom's call a few days ago, Grace knew she needed to fill these two important positions with the absolute best people she could find.

From her vantage point, the rest of the leadership team was hanging in there and doing what they needed to do to improve things. Though she had worried early on that some of them might not make it through the transition, she felt more hopeful about each of them with every passing day.

Grace had also introduced the new mission, vision, and values to her entire leadership team. While some seemed genuinely excited about it, many appeared indifferent.

Though initially disappointed by some of their reactions, Grace knew it would take time to make them clear, tangible, and real. She believed that as she repeated them often and strived to consistently live by them, enthusiasm around them would grow.

The team had also participated in their first few morning huddles. Though the first one had been difficult, Grace saw improvements with the next two and was convinced they were already improving communication and clarity throughout the leadership team and within the center.

Now, despite the progress in some areas, Grace recognized there were still too many customer complaints, too little growth in patient volume, and too many staff members leaving—though that had slowed considerably. So, although there were some signs of improvement, Grace believed it wasn't good enough if she hoped to turn things around quickly. Besides, Tom had made it clear that the board of directors expected to see better results at Wisdom immediately. At this point, she had little hope for any patience or extension of time from them even though she believed they must be aware of the steep mountain they were asking her to climb.

So although some improvements were being made, doubts still lingered that she'd be able to pull it off in time. Though she was convinced that her focus on the four C's model would move the center toward their goals and an eventual transformation, she worried it may not be soon enough.

I hope I'll have enough time.

The Fight

"You need to come back now!" Marshall said over the phone, sounding frantic. Grace had stepped away from the center to attend a meeting with a local physician she had hoped to build a relationship with. She wanted to speak with the doctor about Wisdom's services and encourage him to make referrals to the center.

"What's wrong?" Grace asked, concerned about what might have happened that would require her to return so urgently.

"A fistfight broke out between two staff members at the nurse station on unit three. Several patients and family members were nearby, and many witnessed it. We've separated the two employees, but there is a lot of chaos on the unit, and some concerned family members want answers. Rosie is now handling the staff, and I've tried to reassure the patients and family members. However, one in particular is extremely upset and demanding to speak with you right away. I know you're visiting Dr. Stucky, and I know how important that is, but I wanted to make you aware of what's happened. You may want to come back as soon as you possibly can."

Grace asked if anyone had been hurt, and then she quickly rescheduled her appointment with the physician and headed back to the center. She couldn't help but feel annoyed as she rushed down the road.

I've spent so much time at the center over the last four weeks, and the first time I'm out of it, this happens. Grace tried to fight the small voice in her head that was telling her Wisdom's reputation and poor culture was just too much to overcome. *What kind of health care center has fistfights breaking out among staff members?*

Grace wasn't sure what to expect when she arrived.

Thankfully, no one had been hurt in the incident. Though the details weren't all that interesting, Grace's recently promoted director of nursing services had handled the situation well. She and Rosie took the appropriate actions with the staff members involved, and they were able to smooth over most concerns the patients and family members had had. It seemed everything was going to be OK by the time she made it back.

To Grace, however, this was a clear sign that she needed to do more to push clarity down to the frontline staff. Though it had increased over the last few weeks for her leadership team, she wasn't convinced clarity had changed all that much for the rest of her employees.

After what became infamously labeled as "the fight," Grace knew exactly what her executive team needed to discuss at their next meeting.

Monday Meeting

It was a brisk early spring morning as Grace parked her car in her usual spot behind the health care center. Just like many others, she knew today's executive meeting would be an important one. After the fight that had broken out between two staff members on Friday, she worried the implementation of the four C's model was not going as well as she wanted it to.

"We need to figure out how to push clarity, specifically around our building blocks, to our entire team," Grace said, opening the meeting and introducing the topic for discussion. "We've improved clarity among our leadership team, but more needs to happen for our frontline team members. So today, together, I'd like us to create a plan to increase clarity, focusing on our front line."

The executives then dove into discussing and debating the topic, but they struggled to settle on action items that made sense. After a while, Grace had written only three items they had agreed on thus far on the whiteboard. This is what it looked like.

Wisdom HC's Frontline Clarity Plan

1. Hang a poster of the mission, vision, and values in each break room, as well as the hallway leading to the employee parking lot.
2. Consistently share the mission, vision, and values during every monthly all-staff meeting.
3. Create awards for individuals who live the mission and values.

Looking at the three simple items, Grace realized they should have done at least the first two of them much sooner. Though lamenting the mistake, she realized there was nothing she could do to go back and change the past, so she let it go.

Something else was also bothering her. Though these three items were a good start, she knew they weren't enough. They needed to do more to create clarity throughout their center.

At this point, it seemed the executive team was discouraged by their lack of progress on the topic as well as being distracted by other pressing items. Rather than trying to push forward, they agreed as a group to end their meeting and revisit the topic the following day.

Grace hoped they could figure this out ASAP. She knew it would be critical to their success.

Epiphany

"Another One Bites the Dust" might need to be our new theme song, Grace thought as she walked to her office frustrated late in the afternoon. Rosie had just informed her that another new hire was leaving the organization, and they'd have the same position open once again. Though the staffing crisis had improved, Grace and her leadership team recognized a new problem emerging. Fewer tenured staff were leaving, but the center was having a hard time keeping newly hired employees. The staffing problem seemed to be evolving from simply getting people in the door to now convincing them to stay—and to stay for more than just a few days.

While discussing this specific problem with some of her leadership team members, two interesting things came to light—at least, they seemed interesting to her.

First was the fact that a lot of the people they were hiring were certainly qualified and experienced. By all accounts, they seemed like capable individuals who could perform the job functions. There was no reason to believe that a lack of skill or competence was pushing people away.

Second was the fact that it seemed new hires were having trouble meshing and getting along with the existing team.

Grace sat contemplating how the two observations contributed to the departure of new employees, and neither made sense to her. It seemed that hiring more seasoned and experienced people was the smart choice. And having gotten to know many of the team members on the floor personally over the last month, she genuinely believed that, for the most part, they were pretty good people. And she knew they were certainly interested in having more help on the floor.

Suddenly, Grace had an epiphany and felt she knew why the clarity plan her executive team had discussed earlier in the day felt inadequate. *Our plan must be expanded to new hires. In fact*, she thought, *it needs to expand beyond them to people who are just beginning to inquire about employment with us.*

Grace believed if people learned what their culture was all about the moment they were introduced to Wisdom, it would help that culture to grow. *They must buy into it and commit to living it before we hire them.*

She also recognized that most of her frontline team wasn't living the culture yet. However, if she and her team openly pointed this out and challenged new hires to carry the banner of Wisdom's culture, together they could have a significant impact. She was certain that providing this clarity from the beginning would help them find and hire people who were up to the challenge.

Grace felt convinced this was at least one missing piece to their clarity plan for frontline workers. She wanted to talk to her executive team right away about her thoughts but decided it could wait until their meeting tomorrow.

Tuesday Ad Hoc Meeting

Grace found herself in her familiar spot at the conference room table with her executive team surrounding her. It was funny to Grace how everyone always sat in the same places as if there were assigned seating. She also found it interesting no one ever elected to sit in the empty chair between Jenn and Rosie. This empty seat served as a reminder to them all that leaders were still missing from their team.

Grace brought up the topic everyone expected to be discussing today.

"Our plan to create more clarity with our frontline staff felt insufficient yesterday, and I believe I know at least one reason why. Though we were focused on frontline staff, we didn't consider new hires and people who are just applying to our organization or even just learning about Wisdom."

Most around the table seemed intrigued, so Grace continued.

"If we immerse people in our culture from the beginning and are clear about what we are all about, what matters most to us, and what we are all striving for, and if we own that we aren't where we'd like to be yet and elicit their help in creating the culture we all want, I think we can begin to make real progress with creating clarity for our frontline.

"I've asked Rosie to share a few numbers with us that I think will help everyone see how important this is."

Rosie then presented some sobering turnover numbers for newly hired staff over the last few weeks, and everyone on the team agreed this was something that was missing from their plan.

After an hour-long discussion, the team had added significantly to their clarity plan on the whiteboard. This is what it now looked like.

Wisdom HC's Frontline Clarity Plan

1. Hang a poster of the mission, vision, and values in each break room, as well as the hallway leading to the employee parking lot.
2. Consistently share the mission, vision, and values during every monthly all-staff meeting.
3. Create awards for individuals who live the mission and values.
4. Update the new employee orientation agenda to include a presentation from the CEO on the mission, vision, and values and make this the true focal point throughout the orientation process.
5. Have each employee go through the revamped employee orientation process (both new hires and existing team members).

Interview Process

1. Add an additional page to the employment application. This page will include two essay-style questions: 1) At Wisdom Health Care Center, our mission is to create excellent experiences for each person we serve. Please tell us briefly how you will help us live our mission each day. 2) At Wisdom, our core values are employee committed, ownership, customer care, and greatness. Please tell us how you represent these values.
2. During the interview, each interviewer will first focus on the responses to this additional application page. Ultimately, the center will hire for "fit" to our culture rather than experience. This doesn't mean we don't value experience. It simply means we need people who are excited about our culture and what we are trying to do.
3. The interview process will include a tour of the center, where an interviewer will observe how the candidate interacts with other staff, patients, and visitors. This will help us determine if the candidate truly embraces our values.
4. At the conclusion of an interview, the one-page document with our mission, vision, and values will be given to the candidate.

Grace and the executive team felt more satisfied with their plan. Just as Grace was about to close the meeting, Jenn spoke up. "What if we offered a raise to every new employee who memorized our mission, core values, and vision? I know it sounds crazy, but it seems our team members who really learn these important things would add more value to our center."

Grace's immediate reaction was *no way*, mostly because of the current financial situation the center found itself in. However, rather than blurt out her first thought, she waited to see what others' opinions were. "What does everyone think about this idea?"

Bruce immediately shared he thought it was a bad idea while Rosie thought it was brilliant. Marshall seemed mildly OK with it but didn't seem to have a strong opinion one way or the other.

As Grace considered the opinions of her team, she began to realize how this might more quickly help create clarity and even reinforce some of the other *C*'s like celebration throughout her health care center. *If organizational clarity could be established more quickly by doing this, the investment might actually pay for itself*, she suddenly thought. *It's a risk, but it might be worth it.*

Grace realized that if Wisdom was serious about the mission, vision, and values, then offering raises to those who memorized them would be a powerful way to prove it. As Grace mulled over the idea in her head, her opinion began to shift.

"I really appreciate everyone's candid viewpoints and comments," Grace said, bringing everyone's attention back to her. "They've been helpful. And I'm so thankful we are becoming more comfortable with sharing our honest opinions openly on important matters.

"I'll confess my initial reaction was exactly that of our trusty CFO over there," Grace said, nodding at Bruce.

"But now I'm leaning more toward the opinion of our shrewd VP of HR.

"If offering a raise to new hires and any other employee who memorizes these most important items builds clarity. And if it communicates to people we are serious about this stuff and will be consistent with it. And if it helps them acclimate and add value more quickly than they otherwise would. And if it gives us a chance to increase celebration as people reach this accomplishment. And if it entices even a few team members to stay longer than they otherwise would. And if it makes these individuals champions of our culture. And if it shows we have charity toward our staff by providing a way for them to earn an additional raise outside our normal policies for raises. And if it helps us live our values and mission better and achieve our vision, then this investment will more than pay for itself."

Grace allowed that to sink in for a minute and then finally asked, "Thoughts?"

After some more discussion and careful weighing of the pros and cons, they determined that, though it was a risk, it would be worth a shot in helping them improve the culture and performance of the operation. And although he still had his doubts, Bruce agreed to align with the group and support the idea. Grace recognized this was another concession made by her CFO, and his willingness to get behind her and the others set an excellent example for everyone on the team. She loved that he was working for the betterment of Wisdom as a whole and not just advocating for his own agenda. Grace was grateful and made a mental note to personally thank Bruce. She knew he was having a significant impact and making an important contribution to the team through his actions.

Grace then added one final item to their plan.

6. Offer a 1.5% raise to new hires and any Wisdom team member who memorizes the health care center's values, mission, and vision.

From Grace's perspective, the team left feeling good about what they had come up with to help further improve clarity throughout the entire center.

Some Good News

It had been another volatile week of ups and downs at Wisdom, though the highs seemed to be always better than the last highs and the lows not as low as days gone by. The highlight of the week in Grace's mind was the small celebration they had decided to have earlier in the day.

Overtime hours and staff missing their shifts had been a major problem for as long as Grace could tell, but they had seen some big improvements in both these areas over the last two weeks, and Grace wanted to make sure it didn't go unnoticed. So, at shift change, she and a few of the executive team members positioned themselves by the employee entrance doors and handed out slices of freshly baked pie from the bakery next door, thanking their team members for the improvements that had been made. Most seemed both surprised and thankful for the small act of celebration.

Afterward, Grace had the impression that the atmosphere at Wisdom was slowly evolving and improving. She also noted she was able to proudly call many of the team members by name as she handed them a slice of pie. All of these were good signs of better days ahead.

As Grace sat at her desk reviewing some performance numbers late Friday afternoon, she noticed total customer complaints were lower than the week before, and fewer employees had quit. Unfortunately, customer volume was still at a dangerously low level. She knew she needed to fill the VP of marketing position fast.

Suddenly, her phone rang. Looking at the screen, smudged with what looked like coconut cream, she saw it was Sarah calling.

Sarah was the VP of clinical services candidate Grace had sent an offer letter to about an hour ago. Grace quickly answered the phone, hoping to hear good news.

"Hello, Sarah, how are you?" Grace said as her hands began to sweat a little in anticipation of what she might have to say.

Grace had felt a sense of despair the day her VP of clinical services had walked out the door, but she had soon recognized that it presented her with an opportunity to find a great replacement. And when the VP of clinical services at Northfield strongly recommended Sarah as a potential candidate, she felt both relieved and optimistic.

After her initial conversation with Sarah, Grace was impressed, and in time, she knew she would be a perfect fit for Wisdom.

"I'm good, Grace. I want to thank you for inviting me to attend your little celebration earlier today with your staff. It really told me a lot about you, and I was able to meet some of the team, which was nice. They seemed really great."

"It was great having you here, and I know a few of them were a little forward in asking you lots of difficult questions about how you might handle things if you were in charge. I hope you didn't mind it too much."

Both ladies laughed for a moment.

"No, it was fine. They just want a good boss. I can appreciate that."

Grace was about to say something when Sarah continued, "Anyway, I really was impressed. And so I wanted to let you know I will be accepting your job offer. I look forward to working together."

Grace wanted to shout, "*Yes!*" but instead congratulated Sarah for impressing all the interviewers as well as the staff she'd met during the process.

"And I will be just as committed to the four *C*'s as you are. You've helped me understand and recognize their value."

"You'll be a great leader for this team, Sarah. Thank you for joining us. I'm excited to have you on board."

The two ladies talked through a few specifics, and Grace learned Sarah would be able to start sooner than she had anticipated. After hanging up the phone, she could not have been more elated.

It had been a little over a month since she'd started, and Grace believed momentum was slowly growing. She was convinced that the addition of Sarah would be another huge step in the right direction.

Looking at her notes and the diagram of the four *C*'s model secured to the corner of her desk, Grace knew exactly what she needed to discuss with her executive team during their Monday meeting. At least, that's what she thought.

Not So Fast

Though each passing week seemed to be a little better than the last, this weekend brought back the realities of the challenges the center still faced. Although they had seen improvements over the prior two weeks, many employees didn't show up for their scheduled shifts over the weekend, and the staffing company Wisdom had been using was not helpful in finding replacement workers, even for the contracted staff who never made it in to work.

As a result, Grace and several of her leadership team members had come to work and helped where they could. While at work, many leaders expressed disappointment with the poor attitudes some of their team members displayed while working shorthanded. Grace understood their frustrations, but it only made the unfortunate circumstances worse.

Throughout the day, Grace had questioned if her efforts spent trying to establish the four *C*'s during the last several weeks had really been worth it. After all, they had just celebrated improvements. *And now this*, Grace thought, frustrated. *I know it takes time for the four C's to really help change the culture, but I need changes to happen now!*

Deep down, Grace knew her focus on the four *C*'s had already made a difference and was the right plan. After all, Dan had proved that the four *C*'s worked, and she certainly hadn't come up with any other viable pathway out of the challenges she faced that would lead to sustained results. Still, she couldn't help feeling irritated.

What weighed most heavily on her mind was the lingering staffing crisis and their dependence on contracted staff. *Until we slay that dragon, our ability to make progress will be hampered.*

What had felt like a promising week at Wisdom ended in another long, discouraging weekend.

Bold Proposition

It was Monday morning, and Grace was sitting with her executive team around the conference room table. Two of them had worked most of the weekend with her at the center, and the other two had helped in some capacity remotely. Because of the difficult weekend, Grace had prepared herself for less enthusiasm in the meeting today as well as some possible grumblings.

To her surprise, this wasn't the case. As they began, rather than frustration and exhaustion, she saw anticipation and eagerness in the body language of her team. She sensed each was genuinely looking forward to discussing how to continue to improve results at their center despite the setback. Grace felt grateful for their resolve and a little bothered by her own feelings of doubt and pessimism.

Before Grace could offer her sincere appreciation for everyone's efforts over the weekend, Rosie announced, more to Grace than to anyone else, that she had something to share. Grace noticed she seemed excited but also hesitant.

"Please, go ahead, Rosie."

"Well, ever since we clarified our building blocks, the four of us have been talking a lot."

Grace raised her eyebrows, curious to know what might be coming next. She noticed Rosie hesitate and look around the room at the others before announcing, "We all would really like to go for the Industry Excellence Award. We think we can do it. And we also believe striving to achieve it will help us implement the four *C*'s model we've talked about and are committed to. What do you think?"

Grace was stunned. The Industry Excellence Award was given only to those health care centers that demonstrated excellence in every aspect of their business, from patient satisfaction scores to clinical outcomes, revenue growth, and even employee satisfaction. Grace had become familiar with the award working at Northfield, where they had achieved it more than a couple of times during Dan's tenure as the CEO. In fact, Grace was convinced that because of Northfield's success at winning it multiple times, many operations across Wiser Care, Inc. wanted to follow suit and vigorously pursued the accolade. It had become an annual goal for many of the best centers in the company.

Though it didn't surprise Grace that her team knew about the award and might even be interested in winning it someday, she was surprised to hear Rosie suggesting it, especially after such a difficult weekend. Besides, the center had been a poor performer for so long and was nowhere near reaching any of the stringent requirements needed to win the award. The fact that Wisdom hadn't seen a profitable month for over a year made it an incredibly unlikely candidate. Grace decided Rosie was either crazy or naïve but then concluded it must be both.

Grace tried her best to hide her astonishment when Bruce jumped in. "I know it seems far-fetched for us right now; none of us would deny that. But in the past, I was part of a team that nearly won it. Based on my experience, the journey of just trying to go for it brought our team together. Though it required a lot of work, it was such a great thing for us to shoot for. We don't expect to win the award anytime soon, but it is an honor just to even be known as a center that is striving . . ."

The CFO trailed off, looking directly at Grace with a disappointed look on his face. Grace realized it was probably because of the shocked expression on her own face. Out of everyone in the room, Grace viewed Bruce as the most down-to-earth and logical thinker in the group. She couldn't hide her surprise hearing his take on the idea.

Grace tried to recover as she didn't want to completely shut her team down. Perhaps in some ways, she had underestimated them.

Then, to Grace's further amazement, Jenn quickly chimed in. "We know you won it at Northfield, and we want to win it too. We're tired of being shown up by our sister center across town."

"Not to mention our sister centers across the country," Marshall interrupted.

Jenn then continued, "Besides, we think we have the beginning of the right team to do it here in this room. If we can add two more great leaders to fill our open executive positions, we all believe we can at least make great progress toward accomplishing it."

"And who knows? Maybe one day, we'll actually do it," Rosie added.

Although Rosie had brought it up, it was now clear to Grace that all four of her executive team members had spoken about this at length, and all seemed to believe it was a good idea. She wasn't sure at that moment if she should feel proud or baffled.

While she desperately wanted to believe it might one day be attainable, Grace had serious doubts about Wisdom's ability to ever stack up against her former center or any others that achieved the award. She then imagined herself bringing up this idea to Tom and felt certain he'd instantly burst out laughing at such a notion. *I guess it might give everyone a good chuckle*, Grace thought. She knew to Tom, and to everyone else outside this room for that matter, such an idea would seem absolutely absurd.

Breaking Grace from her thoughts, Rosie added, "Like I mentioned, we think going for the award will at the very least help us bring clarity, consistency, celebration, and maybe even charity to our organization. It will give us clear goals that align our team, it will allow us to consistently move in a direction toward reaching those goals, it will give us a chance to celebrate as we make progress, and I believe it will show we care because we are striving to be the best, even for our employees."

Grace looked at all four of her colleagues as they looked eagerly back at her. She had really grown to enjoy working with them and had to admire their ambition. Ever since the former VP of clinical services and VP of marketing had left, these remaining four had come together and had shown a true desire to improve performance at Wisdom. Grace noticed each seemed hopeful she would agree to the far-fetched idea. She could tell they were serious about it, and based on what Rosie had just said, she could tell they had put a lot of thought into it. This wasn't a spur-of-the-moment idea. *How can I squash their hopes and dreams by saying I think they are absolutely crazy?* Grace thought.

After another second, scarcely believing what was coming out of her own mouth, Grace responded. "OK. OK, let's do it. But here's the deal. We can't let this award distract us from what's most important to us, which is our mission, vision, and values. I'm familiar with the award, yes, and I know its standards are aligned with what we've set out to do with our building blocks, but this award can't overtake them and become our number one priority." All nodded in agreement, and she detected a slight smile on each of their faces.

Grace then added, "Also, even if we fail miserably, we must not let it slow down our momentum or allow it to discourage us. The most important thing right now is establishing the C's and, specifically at this time, clarity."

Again, everyone agreed as Jenn shook hands with Rosie as if congratulating her on her pitch.

Then, without thinking, Grace added, "And when we win it, we can't let it go to our heads either."

Some of the leaders in the room almost cheered as Grace smiled, thinking about their complete and utter audacity.

In that moment, she felt more hope rising among the executive team and even allowed herself to wonder if perhaps they could achieve this goal someday at Wisdom. The truth was it had been something she had dreamed about achieving as a CEO one day. It had just never crossed her mind it could happen at Wisdom.

Grace and her team continued their meeting with a brief discussion about the award, in which she confessed openly she thought they were crazy. She also expressed she was grateful for their confidence and, most importantly, for their desire to live true to their mission and achieve their vision.

The executives then reviewed their miserable weekend, the staffing crisis, and potential candidates for the open VP of marketing position.

Though the topics of the meeting were nothing that she had wanted to talk about when she had left her office Friday evening, the miserable weekend had changed everything. She knew it was probably best to wait until next week's meeting before introducing the topic she had intended to discuss. Besides, she believed this week's meeting had already centered a lot on how they could continue to work on implementing the four *C*'s model. She knew this was what they needed to continue to concentrate on most to continue to improve their culture.

Despite the unexpected meeting topics, overall, Grace felt it had been another effective meeting. And the unified and bold proposition offered by her executive team made her believe they were coming together more quickly than she had anticipated.

More Clarity

Another week had gone by, and Grace found herself in front of her executive team again.

"Thanks, everyone, for being here this morning. It's good to be back together again under better circumstances after a much smoother weekend than the last one we endured. I think it's fair to say most of us are feeling a little fresher today than we did a week ago." Grace said this with a smile, and a few nodded their heads and smiled in return.

"We've begun to clarify the building blocks of our culture, which is a really good start, but now we need to become more clear about other important items. Specifically, I'd like us to develop clarity around our collective goals as a health care center."

Over the next hour and a half, Grace and her team discussed and debated what their center's goals should be, especially in conjunction with their mission, vision, and values. Since her team had brought it up in last week's meeting, Grace realized that the Industry Excellence Award criteria gave them a good resource to base many of their team goals on. She was now feeling even more grateful her team had so boldly brought it up. She recognized it would help them in new ways to further establish each of the *C*'s.

After about an hour and a half, the team came away with twelve collective monthly goals they would strive to achieve as an entire center. The goals ranged from patient satisfaction scores, census growth, and clinical outcomes to employee safety, cash collections, and employee turnover.

They also discussed a plan for how they would consistently track and measure the goals and how they would communicate results frequently to others. This is what Grace wrote down for their goal-tracking plan.

Wisdom HC's Goal-Tracking Plan

1. Create a simple scoreboard listing all 12 goals.
2. Post copies of the scoreboard in all leadership conference rooms and employee break rooms.
3. Update scoreboards posted throughout the center at the beginning of each month.
4. Review goals weekly and discuss progress and opportunities during weekly leadership meeting.
5. Review goals monthly and discuss progress during monthly all-staff meetings.

The executive team then decided to introduce the goals to their entire team, creating a similar plan to the one they used to introduce the mission, vision, and values, starting first at the next daily huddle with their leadership team and then informing the rest of their team at the next all-staff meeting.

With creating clarity around goals, Grace and her executive team hoped to see steady growth and progress toward reaching all twelve of them throughout the rest of the year.

Grace also knew the consistent tracking and posting of progress toward their goals would not only help them establish clarity, but also reinforce the second C— consistency—which was something she had been thinking about more and more.

By this point as the leader at Wisdom, Grace felt good about the steps she and the team were taking toward establishing clarity. She believed their efforts were improving their center's culture in a significant way, but the constant worry of the short time frame she was working under was never far from her mind.

Disappointment

This is worse than I expected, Grace thought as she looked at her center's monthly financial reports. Because she had started at Wisdom several days into March, April was the first month in which Grace felt the results rested entirely on her shoulders. This is how the net income graphs had turned out.

Wisdom Health Care Net Income $

Grace was frustrated to see that Wisdom's streak of yet another month of losses had continued. Though she believed good things were happening, the financial performance of the health care center did not reflect them in any way.

As she studied the financial reports, she could see revenue was well below where she knew it needed to be, and though she had made adjustments to staffing and had improved other expenses, it hadn't been enough. Much to Grace's chagrin, the center was also still struggling with filling open positions, so they continued to spend an exorbitant amount on contracted staff.

On paper, Grace was extremely disappointed with the lack of progress she'd made during her first seven weeks as the center's CEO. It was hard for her not to question whether she was on the right track and if the four *C*'s model was having as much of an impact as she had thought.

Grace's biggest concern about the disappointing results revolved around the conversation she'd had with Tom many weeks ago. How would Tom and the Wiser Care, Inc. board respond to this loss? Would they view it as an indictment of her ability to eventually turn the health care center around?

Surely, they'll give me more time, she thought. *No reasonable person could expect an operation that has been struggling for so many years to have a sudden drastic turnaround overnight, right?*

Discouraged and worried, Grace decided it might be helpful to schedule a meeting with Dan.

* * *

When Dan met with Grace in her office the following day, she began to feel better but not completely comforted.

Though the monthly performance metrics in April at Wisdom were about what they had been for the last two years, Dan reminded her that being a CEO and leading a successful team was more of a marathon than a sprint. And that establishing each of the *C*'s took not only diligence but also patience. He then reminded her that anything she did to improve clarity, consistency, celebration, and charity would always help her situation, but it didn't mean instant results.

He also told her he was certain that, as she continued to focus on the *C*'s, their impact would be felt sooner than she might expect. He was convinced she shouldn't try to take any shortcuts that might undermine her ability to achieve long-term success at Wisdom.

Finally, Dan reassured her there was no better way to turn things around than trusting the model and instilling each of the *C*'s firmly at Wisdom. His conviction about what the four *C*'s model could do for her and how it would truly help her come out on top in the end if she stuck with it was just the encouragement she needed.

As Dan gathered up his belongings and prepared to leave, he casually commented, "You know, Grace, I could feel a real difference here today. As I opened the door and walked through the halls, there was just a different vibe than what I usually get here at Wisdom. I can't put my finger on it, other than the staff seemed different, almost like they had a sense of pride being here rather than feeling ashamed."

"Thank you, Dan."

Though he didn't know it, these last comments meant the world to Grace, especially at a time when she was questioning her effectiveness as a leader. She had believed there was a different ambience permeating the center, but she also worried it might be self-created by her own hopeful and biased perspective.

In the end, Grace was grateful for Dan's visit, and she recommitted herself to doing all she could to establish the *C*'s at Wisdom.

Part Two

Consistency and Charity

The Review

It's time to focus more on consistency, Grace thought as she sat in her office alone early one morning. *And I think I have an idea of where to start.*

During her time working under Dan, he had consistently held a monthly review on many key metrics with his entire leadership team. She had always looked forward to this review as a leader in his center, and now she knew she needed to implement the same practice at Wisdom.

With her mind squarely focused on the four *C*'s model, she recognized this monthly practice not only helped Dan establish consistency but also provided more clarity and even added opportunities for celebration. Though Wisdom's numbers had been a disappointment in April, she knew it was time to start this monthly tradition.

Without forewarning, Grace was standing in front of her entire leadership team going through April's results. She first reviewed the twelve collective team goals they had just introduced. Next, she showed how each specific department did with their spending in comparison to the established goals, as well as in comparison to the center's historic monthly spending. Then she went through important clinical metrics and finally ended with the net income results. It was a comprehensive review that she knew would leave little doubt in anyone's mind about the highs and lows of their performance.

During her presentation, Grace sensed some leaders in the room were feeling a little uncomfortable. She decided it was probably due to one of two things. Either they were feeling uneasy simply by the amount of transparency she was providing around the center's performance, or perhaps they might be feeling exposed because of how their departments were being portrayed in front of their peers. Regardless of the reason, she was confident this consistent practice would reinforce many of the *C*'s in the model.

"Thank you for allowing me this time to review our month's performance. I do want you to know this will become a tradition of ours; we will review our performance each month together like this, although we will probably go into even more depth next time."

Grace noticed a few eyebrows raised with that comment.

"I want us to not only compare our numbers to our own monthly goals and historic performance, but I'd also like to compare our results to our sister center across town."

Grace noticed another round of rising eyebrows in the room and even heard what sounded like a slight gasp. She realized it probably seemed outrageous to compare Wisdom's numbers to Northfield's, but to become the best, she felt they needed to see comparisons to the best.

She went on. "This will give us good benchmarks of where we'd like to be and what we hope to become. Each month, I will specifically point out where it looks like we are doing well and where the numbers show we are struggling. And I'd like this to be more interactive, where we stop and have some brief discussion as a group on how we can improve and do better."

Grace stopped talking, and the room was silent for a moment. She wasn't sure what her team members were thinking and was about to ask when Bruce finally spoke up.

"I really like the idea of reviewing performance across the board like this. Seeing these numbers together will help us all have more clarity on our results. Each of us will know exactly how we are doing and where we stand with established goals."

"I think it will invite us to work together better as well," Marshall offered, "and pinpoint areas where we are struggling so we all can help out. Since I've been here at Wisdom, we've never reviewed the numbers like this before as an entire leadership team. This will be good for us."

"I agree," Jenn then added. "I normally just review my own department's numbers alone. So although I always know how my individual department is performing, I've never really been apprised of how others are doing. It was interesting to see how the spending in our dietary department has really gone up, for example. I would never have known that, but now that I have this information, I wonder if there's more I can be doing to help with this."

"I agree. This will be really good for us," Rosie added, and with that, most in the room were now nodding.

Grace was elated that her executive team members had chimed in and put their support behind her. She could tell that everyone in the room now seemed on board with the new practice.

"Thank you," Grace said sincerely, adding, "the reason why we will do this monthly is because I believe it will help us improve our results. It will provide clarity around goals, budgets, and performance that we haven't had among this leadership group before. And it will give us reasons to celebrate when we see we're making progress and doing well.

"I also believe as leaders in this center you deserve to know where we stand in all aspects of our business. True to our core values, we all should be acting like owners of Wisdom Health Care Center, and owners are in the know when it comes to company results.

"Most importantly, though," Grace paused for a few seconds to make sure everyone was still listening before adding, "I believe doing this will help us live our mission and achieve our vision."

With that, Grace turned off the projector and flipped on the lights. She was thinking about how best to wrap things up when Sarah, who had only started a day before, spoke up for the first time during the review.

"Can I say I love this? And I just learned so much about this place on my second day here. I can't wait to see how these numbers improve with each passing month. I'm confident we can surpass our established goals and even exceed the performance of our sister center across town."

Grace could not have planned for a better way to close their first comprehensive monthly review as a team.

More Charity

Grace was thrilled to have her new VP of clinical services on board. After only three days, Grace could tell Sarah was having an impact.

Grace decided to add her name and what she knew about her to the executive team list she had created.

> Sarah, VP of clinical services—experienced leader with good clinical knowledge and strong people skills. Likes to camp and go to the lake with her family. Has one son and one daughter. Her husband, Rick, is a high school science teacher. Grew up in a large family, many of whom live in the area.

There is still a lot more I need to get to know about her, Grace thought as she looked at what she had written. Grace then took a few minutes to add some of the personal things she had learned about the other executive team members over the last month and a half to her list.

> Marshall, COO—young and new to his role as COO. Has worked at the center for only a few months. Appears to be trying but is struggling in the role. Does seem like a hard worker. **Was recruited out of Seattle, WA, by Wiser Care, Inc. to specifically come help Wisdom. He likes sports and has a**

competitive nature. He's engaged to be married and has wedding plans for the end of the year.

Jenn, VP of rehabilitation—has worked at Wisdom for two years, but it hasn't been smooth. Has openly shared she has considered leaving Wisdom because of the instability and poor clinical care. Is blunt and almost rude and wears her emotions on her sleeve. Seems to really know her stuff and appears to be respected by others in the center. *Loves dogs. She has three dogs currently and would like more. Her husband is a loan officer at Union Bank, and they have a thirteen-year-old son attending Lakeport Middle School.*

Bruce, CFO—is on his second stint with the center. Worked at Wisdom many years ago but left to work for a nearby competitor. Returned about nine months ago. Has good experience as a CFO. Though cleanup is still needed, there have been good improvements in the business office's performance metrics since his return. Business office results seem to be the only metrics trending in the right direction currently. Seems organized and methodical. *Is married with three daughters. The oldest two are in college while the youngest is a senior in high school. He is a proud Aggie and likes to be involved with his alma mater, where his oldest daughter attends.*

Rosie, VP of HR—the veteran in the group. Very self-confident. Has worked at Wisdom for more than twenty years in various positions. Is a wealth of knowledge about anything to do with the center

124

*and seems to be well known throughout it. Has been the only dependable and constant leadership person. Seems to have surprising loyalty to Wisdom despite its many challenges. **Has four grown children and several grandchildren she loves to visit. Also likes to cook and is an avid follower and fan of the local sports teams. She is also involved at the church she attends. Her faith is very important to her.***

After adding more details, Grace admired the names of the people she had gotten to know better over the last seven and a half weeks. She genuinely felt excited to continue to learn more about each of them and add to her growing list.

She suddenly felt grateful that each individual leader on the list seemed just as committed as she was to the four *C*'s model. Because of it, Grace felt the momentum at Wisdom building more and more.

Census Questions

Grace felt her phone vibrating, and looking, she saw it was Tom. "I need to take this," she said stepping out of a clinical review meeting.

"Hello, Tom," Grace said, answering the phone.

"Hi, Grace," Tom said, then quickly added, "have you looked at your census numbers lately? It seems the place is falling apart."

Grace instinctively rolled her eyes and felt like giving him a piece of her mind, but instead, she calmly answered, "Yes, Tom, I'm aware our patient volume is low. I can assure you we are focused on improving census daily."

Grace thought she could hear Tom sigh before he said, "How's it coming with that VP of marketing candidate?"

"Spencer hasn't seen the light yet, but I'm sure he'll be coming to his senses soon," Grace answered, hoping that would be the end of the discussion.

"I don't know, Grace. I think it may be time to hire someone else. Your numbers can't keep dropping, and you can't do it all by yourself. What about that other candidate you interviewed and sort of liked? He was interested, right? Why not go ahead and give him a shot?"

Though the thought had crossed her mind many times, Grace knew if she wanted to attract the best people, then she had to hire the best. She was convinced Spencer was not only skilled at what he did but would also be the best fit for the culture they were trying to build at Wisdom. She wasn't going to settle.

"Tom, you know how important this role is, and how critical it is I fill it with the right person. You of all people know I have little leeway for a mistake on this one. Spencer is our top choice without question, so I'll be patient until he comes around, or we find someone even better."

"Well, honestly, I'm worried."

"I'm confident I can eventually win him over. And in the meantime, my entire team is rallying around our need to improve census. We'll stay on it until the right leader can join us."

Tom didn't respond for a moment, and Grace thought he would drop the subject. She was wrong.

"Come on, Grace, let's look at this logically. Do you think Spencer will come? I mean, with the shape the center has been in and the reputation it has out there, I just don't think it's realistic that you can land the top guy. It's probably wise to hire whoever you can get at this point and then do the best you can with what you have."

Grace had to take a moment to calm down again before she answered.

In her mind, she envisioned sarcastically thanking Tom for the state the health care center was in when she started. She knew, however, this wouldn't help anything. Instead, she said with conviction, "I will not settle. If I hire the wrong person, you and I both know Wisdom will be doomed. Besides, what we're trying to accomplish here is too important. We'll be relentless in pursuing the best people so we can have the best outcomes. Our mission and vision for this place demands that. Period."

Though Grace didn't share it with Tom, she also knew hiring Spencer would reinforce clarity and consistency among her team. They would see Grace was serious about not settling and wanting to hire only the best or at least those who they felt were the best fit for their team.

This was a message she had preached to them over the last couple of weeks, and she couldn't go back on it now. It would be confusing if she hired someone else because, up to that point, the only person they had all agreed on was Spencer.

"All right, Grace," Tom said, finally relenting. "Please let me know if there is anything I can do to help get Spencer on board ASAP."

"Will do, Tom." And with that, Grace hung up.

Though feeling slightly stressed about her decision to wait before hiring someone, Grace was certain she was doing the right thing. She knew that bringing on the wrong person could hurt the culture and results at Wisdom. She and her team were unified in their belief that Spencer was the best fit thus far. Now she only needed Spencer to come around sooner rather than later.

"So how do you plan to convince Spencer to join such an awful health care center?" Rosie said from the doorway.

"You heard that?" Grace asked, surprised to see Rosie standing there.

"Yes, I did. Sounds like your boss is worried. He asked a fair question, you know. Do you really think Spencer will join us based on our reputation?"

Grace could sense doubt in Rosie's question and decided it was a great opportunity to reinforce clarity around their vision and where the center was headed.

"The way I'm going to convince Spencer to join us is to tell him about our mission and vision. We're doing something special here, Rosie. In time, we'll become the center others look to, learn from, and aspire to become. We'll even surpass Dan's building."

Grace saw Rosie's eyebrows rise. "Who wouldn't want to be a part of this? Who doesn't want to be part of the most successful turnaround in the company? And be a part of a team that will leave a lasting impact on the industry? We're doing big things here. And this will have a big effect on each person who's a part of it. I'd hate for him to miss this opportunity. I'm convinced he's better off here than anywhere else.

"Now we just have to help him see that."

"All right, all right, I'm convinced too," Rosie responded as she raised her hands in front of her with a smile. "I have no more doubts, I promise. And with that speech, a person would be a fool not to join us."

Both ladies laughed as Grace relaxed. "Our building blocks are so important. And holding true to them will be what separates us from others. We have big plans here and an exciting vision. When we believe in it, talk about it, and work toward it, honestly, who wouldn't want to be a part of it?"

Rosie nodded, and Grace felt she had made her point. She only hoped Spencer would make the choice to join them soon.

The Test

"Hello, everyone," Grace said to her team of executives who were gathered around the conference room table as she entered the room. "Today we need to get down to business immediately. We need to talk again about our dwindling census numbers. I know we've had a lot of discussion about this lately, but how do we grow our patient volume quickly? Any thoughts?"

The executive team members looked around at one another and then finally, Jenn offered, "You know, I've been thinking. Why do we need such a thorough screening and authorization process to admit someone to our health care center? It seems sometimes we lose customers because we are too slow to respond. What if we allowed anyone on the executive team to approve any potential patient without having to go through our current process, which is slow and cumbersome? I know we've lost opportunities because of how long it takes us to review all the information and respond with a yes or no to a potential admission."

Grace thought about it and could see Jenn had a point.

"What does everyone else think?"

As Grace looked around the room, most heads were nodding.

Finally, Bruce said, "I don't know. I mean, we still need to verify benefits. That can't be taken out of the process. The last thing we want to do is fill our beds with people who are unable to pay."

"But what if the person who received the referral had the responsibility to check and verify the benefits and then respond to the referral rather than having to reach out to your team?" Jenn responded.

"That would avoid having to track people down and interrupt them. As of now, someone on your team has to stop in the middle of what they are doing to verify benefits on every single potential admission. Removing this could make the approval process much more efficient," Jenn added.

"I'm not sure I'm totally clear about this," responded Grace.

"Is the thought that when one of us receives the referral, we then have the responsibility to verify benefits and approve the patient to be admitted without getting others involved at all? If so, we'd all need access to the benefits verification system as well as some training to make sure we knew what we were looking at."

"Yes," responded Jenn. "I think that would work, and I'd love to learn something new."

"That would definitely speed up our response time, which might really help us improve our census," Marshall added. "I agree we've lost patients because of our current process. I've seen it firsthand."

"Anyone else have thoughts?" Grace asked.

"I like the idea of not having to stop what I am doing a couple of times a day to review a potential new admission," stated Sarah. "If I could trust the person looking over the clinical information and nursing needs of the patient, it would free up my time too."

"I really like this idea. You know referral sources have always been asking for us to speed up our process in getting back to them. And the quicker we respond, the more likely they'll be to use us again. I'm surprised we haven't focused on this sooner. It seems like a no-brainer," added Marshall.

Grace still wasn't sure she understood the details of what the new admission review process would look like.

"To make sure I understand this correctly, we're saying anyone in this room can receive and approve a referral without input from others. Each of us will be given access and training on the benefits verification program as well as what to look for on the clinical side of things. So each of us will share the responsibility of approving and responding to admission inquiries in hopes it will make our response time quicker. Is that right?"

"Yes. And the good thing about sharing this responsibility is if one of us is busy, then the one or two of us who are less busy can handle it. We won't have to wait around for others," Jenn added.

"Are we all in agreement this is a good idea?" Grace asked, looking around the room, feeling unsure.

She noticed most heads were nodding, yet something about the proposed plan didn't seem right. She spotted her notes on the four C's model on the other side of the room and then had an idea.

"OK, before we put a stamp of approval on this process, let's put it through the four C's test." She noticed a few confused faces and smiled. "Don't worry. I haven't explained this test to you yet. It's something I've actually just thought about.

"If we are serious about the four C's model and establishing each C within our center, then any changes we make to processes, programs, policies, and systems should be able to pass the four C's test. Otherwise, we need to refine our decisions until they do."

Rosie then asked the million-dollar question Grace was sure was on everyone's mind. "So what is the four C's test?"

Grace responded, "Any change or any decisions we make should increase clarity, consistency, celebration, or charity in our organization. That doesn't mean the decision or change has to improve all of them, but it must help us reinforce or establish at least one of them."

Grace noticed most heads nodding. "And no change or decision we make should ever take away from our ability to provide clarity, establish consistency, add celebration, or show charity. If it does, we need to tweak our decision until it doesn't. If we hope to turn this place around, we have to be certain we're only making decisions that help us reinforce the four *C*'s and in no way detract from them."

Bruce asked, "So if I understand correctly, the test is really asking two simple questions. The first is 'Will the changes to our admissions approval process help us establish any of the *C*'s in the model?' and the second is 'Will it hurt our ability to establish any of the *C*'s?'"

"Exactly," Grace responded. "Those are the two questions we must ask and answer in order to put our decisions to the four *C*'s test."

"What about our building blocks?" questioned Marshall. "Shouldn't they come into play in some way here?"

Grace could not have been prouder of her COO at that moment. It was a great question.

"Great catch, Marshall. You're right. There should be one final question we must answer to complete the test, and that is 'Is this change aligned with our mission, vision, and values?'"

"So it's three questions, rather than two?" Bruce asked.

"Yes, thanks to Marshall, it is. So let's put this new admissions process through the three questions, or what we can now call the four *C*'s test."

The team sat in silence for a moment, thinking about the changes they had discussed for the admission approval process. Finally, Jenn broke the silence. "This isn't going to work, is it?"

Grace was surprised it was Jenn who first chimed in since she was the one who had initially brought up the idea and seemed to really be pushing it along.

"This is going to cause confusion. If referral sources are getting information and responses from me and then the next day from Bruce and then the next day from Marshall, they'll be confused." Jenn paused as if gathering her thoughts before adding, "They are accustomed to having one point of contact here. I know this is what they like because otherwise, they won't know who they are supposed to talk to when they have questions or need answers because it could be any of us."

"I worry it may lead to inconsistency in how we respond to them as well," Sarah added. "Though on the surface, it seems we'd be able to respond much quicker, what happens when all of us are really busy?"

"Us? Busy? Never," Bruce said sarcastically.

"Or what if one of us assumes someone else is handling it, and then it falls through the cracks. We may respond promptly one time but then not respond at all the next time. We all have a lot on our plates already. This would be something easy to push aside in hopes that someone else would pick it up," Marshall said.

"I'll add that it might result in inconsistency with the kinds of admissions we accept as well," Jenn responded, and Sarah nodded.

After a few more moments, Bruce said, seriously now, "This plan clearly seems to put clarity and especially consistency at risk. Although it will theoretically speed up our process, which I agree could help us improve census. We desperately need to generate more revenue here ASAP."

"Having a little less clarity and consistency might be a sacrifice we need to be willing to make in order to push up patient volume right now, right?" Rosie said, sounding unsure.

134

Grace wanted to jump in but decided to wait to see how others would respond. Her patience paid off.

"I think we can speed up our current process while also reinforcing clarity and consistency. The plan we came up with is clearly flawed, but that doesn't mean we can't find ways to improve it while also establishing the four C's," Marshall offered.

Grace again was impressed with Marshall's comment. She wanted to agree right away but refrained again, waiting to see how others might respond.

"I think Marshall is right," commented Sarah, and now everyone was nodding, including Bruce.

"Thank you, everyone. And I agree with what has been said. This process sounds good in theory, but it would really hurt our ability to be consistent and even clear, which is so important for us right now," Grace stated. "Your input has been excellent, and I appreciate everyone's participation in this important discussion.

"Jenn brought up a great point that we really need to improve and speed up our admissions review process, and Marshall is right. I know we can figure out how to do it in a way that helps us establish the four C's and doesn't take away from them. Did you have anything in mind, Marshall, for how we can do both?"

The team then had more discussion on how they could improve their admission review process in a way that would not only help them respond more quickly to potential admissions but also promote the four C's. In the end, they came up with a plan that included shifting responsibilities so that one person on their broader leadership team could take complete ownership of it and have it as the primary function of their role.

They also made plans to train this person on the benefit verification system and empower them to make quick clinical decisions when feasible to streamline the process. Finally, the plan included new ways they would track response times and evaluate overall effectiveness of the admission approval system more closely.

Most importantly, by the end of the meeting, the executive team came away with a plan that not only improved and sped up the process but also passed the four *C*'s test.

* * *

Later that afternoon, Grace typed out the four *C*'s test she and the team had followed earlier in the day.

The Four *C*'s Test

If we are serious about creating a high-performing company culture, then we must always put our decisions through the four *C*'s test by answering the following questions:

1. Will this decision help reinforce and establish at least one of the four *C*'s (clarity, consistency, celebration, or charity)?
         Yes   No

2. Are we confident that this decision will *not* impede our ability to establish or reinforce any of the four *C*'s (clarity, consistency, celebration, or charity)?
         Yes   No

3. Is this decision aligned with our core values, mission, and vision?
         Yes   No

If our team can confidently answer yes to all three questions, then we know the decision we are making will help elevate our center's culture.

Grace was convinced that any decisions that were able to pass the test would help them improve their culture at Wisdom while any decision they made that didn't pass it would hurt their culture.

On her drive home from work that evening, Grace decided to make a call.

"Brilliant," Dan responded after Grace had explained what had happened that day and how her new test had helped them make a wise decision. "I absolutely love it. It seems so simple yet effective. I'm surprised I never thought of something like this test myself."

Grace smiled, feeling good that she had helped add a tool to Dan's repertoire of systems and practices to establish the four *C*'s.

"I'm sure you've always thought about changes in this way. Putting this simple test on paper just helps me have a more formal process to follow. And from now on, we're going to put all our decisions to the four *C*'s test at Wisdom. I want to ensure everything we do helps establish the *C*'s and doesn't take away from them. I know being consistent with this practice will help us build a strong culture."

"I'll be doing the same here at Northfield," Dan said. He added, "Thanks so much for sharing the four *C*'s test with me, Grace. I'll be sharing it with others as well."

"You better!" Grace replied, smiling.

Another Month's Results

Another full month had gone by, and Grace found herself feeling extremely disappointed once again. She was reviewing the key metrics from their previous month's performance, and results had only marginally improved. She realized that with these results, the sale of Wisdom might soon be inevitable. She felt sick to her stomach.

Though revenue and the number of customers served had picked up somewhat, it had happened too late in the month. Also, some unexpected costs kept them from dramatically improving their bottom line once again. This is how the net income chart turned out for Wisdom in May.

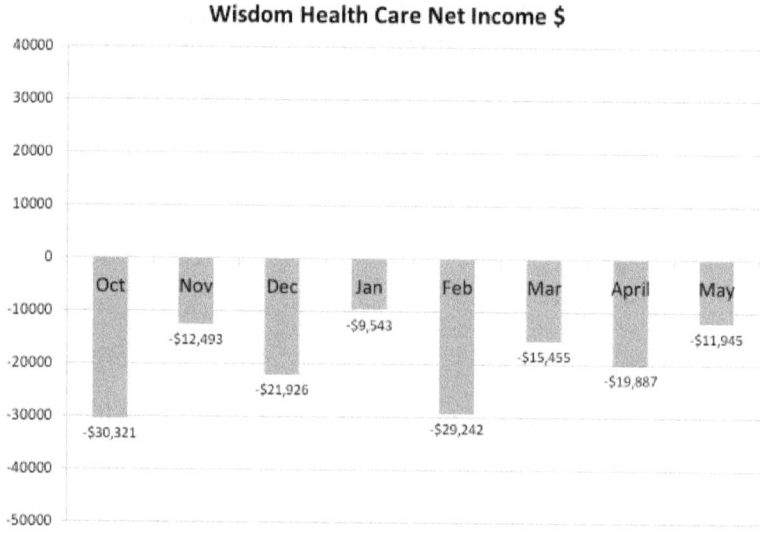

It was hard to see much positive when staring at the net income results; however, many of her leadership team members had asked her about their month's results as well as when they would have their monthly review of key metrics. This was a good sign that her team members were becoming more engaged and were interested in improving.

Though she imagined many would be disappointed by the numbers, she had little doubt that only a few months ago, many on her team wouldn't have cared to know. This signified important progress to her.

* * *

The monthly review felt frustrating to Grace, mostly because she knew how hard the team had worked yet the results were still poor. There were, however, many positive aspects she recognized during it.

First, more questions and discussions had taken place. Almost everyone seemed genuinely interested in seeing and learning more about the numbers.

Second, Grace had noticed fewer people appearing uneasy during the review. She sensed more of them becoming comfortable with having their department's results shared openly with others.

Finally, it felt to her like more on her team were taking ownership of their collective results at the center rather than only being interested in the results for their individual departments.

So, although disappointing, there were signs of hope and improvement Grace couldn't deny. *If I'm given the time to see it through*, Grace thought. "If" was the big question that was never far from her mind.

As Grace turned the lights in the conference room back on and shut off the projector, Bruce said, "Well, that was a little brutal, but it was good to see our number of patients growing right at the end of the month. Our revenue is having a big impact on our financial results, but if we can continue that trend, it will help us a lot for June."

"And recent customer satisfaction scores are looking a lot better too," Marshall added. "This will help us grow our volume."

"And don't forget the improvements in employee turnover," Rosie commented.

Sarah added, "And customer complaints have slowed down considerably."

Grace realized she had probably been too focused on the bad metrics during her review.

"Thanks for pointing those important highlights out, everyone. I probably focused a little too much on only the month's poor outcomes," Grace said apologetically. "These items you've pointed out are good leading indicators for better performance to come across the board, including financially. If we can continue on the path we are on, great things will happen."

If, if, if. If we have the time! Grace clamored to herself, again feeling immense pressure, knowing what the others in the room didn't know.

"Thank you, everyone, for all your efforts during the month of May," Grace added, trying to smile and sound as sincere as possible.

* * *

As Grace sat reflecting on the month's performance metrics again later that evening, she was grateful her executive team members had pointed out the good. Though financial numbers were poor in May, many important metrics had improved.

Grace decided that there were also other, less noticeable things that were beginning to happen that would bode well for their turnaround financially. For example, her team seemed to be gelling like never before, and local physicians were also getting more involved at the center. Additionally, and perhaps most significantly, they had finally eliminated the need for contracted staff. As of that day, every person working in the center was a Wisdom Health Care Center employee. This was a huge accomplishment.

Lastly, Grace recognized within herself that she personally had come a long way as a leader and as the CEO at Wisdom. By consistently adhering to her charity habits, she had grown to genuinely love Wisdom and the people who worked there. She felt a tremendous amount of loyalty and obligation toward her team, and though she never would have guessed it, Grace legitimately looked forward to walking through the center's doors each morning.

Though she had felt down about some of the poor financial results and the meager net income improvement over last month, she surprisingly and suddenly felt a lot of hope. Looking at the net income chart again, Grace prayed she would have enough time to prove the four *C*'s model was working at Wisdom.

Almost as if on cue, Grace's phone began to ring.

"Hello, Tom," Grace said, adding, "any updates on our timeline?"

"No, nothing new. I'm expecting we have very little time before the wheels really go into motion and we formally begin the preliminary steps of selling the center."

This was not what Grace wanted to hear. "What does a little time mean? I'd like to know."

"Maybe two months, three at the most."

"There's still time to change their minds about all this, right?" Grace was worried. When she didn't get an immediate response and heard Tom hesitating, she added, "Look, Tom, I know the numbers still don't show much improvement, but I can assure you with all the confidence I have that things are greatly improving here. If we can have only a few more months to prove ourselves, I know things here at Wisdom will turn around.

"In fact, I'm so confident about it, I'd put my job on the line for it." Though she did feel more assured in the eventual turnaround of the center than ever before, Grace could hardly believe what she had just said. She held her breath for a moment, wondering how Tom might react.

After a moment, Grace heard Tom sigh again as he said, "I'm surprised you feel so confident right now."

Grace gathered her composure and tried to calm down. She did not want to be angry, but at this point, how could she not be? Her only desire was to help Wisdom succeed, and she had given it her all.

With a growing resolve, she finally responded, "I do feel that confident. Turning around a center that has struggled for so long takes time, and I've only been at it for a little more than two and a half months now. Though most of the key metrics our company focuses on don't show it yet, there are signs of improvement all around, I can assure you. For example, we've finally eliminated contracted staff, customer complaints are way down, employee turnover has improved, and morale is at an all-time high."

"But the numbers, Grace. The numbers aren't improving like I had hoped they would."

Grace paused for a moment, wondering if Tom was actually listening to what she was saying before adding, "It would be a big mistake for Wiser Care to sell this operation prematurely."

After another moment, Tom responded flatly, "I hope you're right that things are about to improve, because time is running out." He then added, "But don't worry. As I told you before, we'll find a spot for you within the organization when we sell the center."

"*If* we sell the center, not *when*," Grace corrected.

"Yes, that's right. If we sell the center. No final decisions have been made yet. But all eyes will be on this next month's performance. There needs to be solid improvement to results that we all can see. Without it, I'm afraid the sale of Wisdom will become unavoidable."

"There will be," Grace said without hesitation.

"OK, Grace. Well, good luck. I'm rooting for you. Turning around Wisdom would truly be a remarkable achievement."

"Thanks, Tom."

Grace blew out a big breath of air as she hung up the phone. She was upset that Tom only seemed to be taking their net income results into consideration and believed he was clueless about all that had transpired over the last two and a half months at Wisdom.

Grace knew this month had to be her breakthrough. The four *C*'s had to start producing bottom-line results immediately!

Leadership Update

"He's here!" the receptionist told Grace, sounding excited over the phone. She knew the whole team had been looking forward to this day.

"I'm so glad you're here," Grace said as she extended her hand to Spencer. "We're all thrilled to have you on board."

"I'm ready to get going," Spencer said with a smile. "Let's see if we can't bring those volume numbers up quickly. After all, we will need to if we want to leave a lasting impact on the industry and become a center others aspire to become."

"Very true."

Grace was thrilled her executive team was finally whole. She knew having a complete team would help accelerate their turnaround. Now that Spencer had started, Grace wanted to take some time to update her executive team list.

Spencer, VP of marketing—well connected in the area. Is driven, outgoing, and lots of fun to be around. Has confidence but is not overbearing. Have yet to meet someone who doesn't like him. Likes to sing and plays the guitar, drums, and other instruments.

Though Grace had spent quite a bit of time with Spencer during the recruitment process, she realized she had a lot more to learn about him. She then decided to add the new items she had discovered about the rest of her team.

Marshall, COO—young and new to his role as COO. Has worked at the center for only a few months. Appears to be trying but is struggling in the role. Does seem like a hard worker. Was recruited out of Seattle, WA. by Wiser Care, Inc. to specifically come help Wisdom. He likes sports and has a competitive nature. He's engaged to be married and has wedding plans for the end of the year. *Is a health nut and usually refuses sweets. Favorite sport is basketball. Has plans to get married December 26 by his fiancé's father who is a minister.*

Jenn, VP of rehabilitation—has worked at Wisdom for two years, but it hasn't been smooth. Has openly shared she has considered leaving Wisdom because of the instability and poor clinical care. Is blunt and almost rude and wears her emotions on her sleeve. Seems to really know her stuff and appears to be respected by others in the center. Loves dogs. She has three dogs currently and would like more. Her husband is a loan officer at Union Bank, and they have a thirteen-year-old son attending Lakeport Middle School. *Likes to garden and mows her own lawn. Also loves candy—Sour Patch Kids are her favorite.*

Bruce, CFO—is on his second stint with the center. Worked at Wisdom many years ago but left to work for a nearby competitor. Returned about nine months ago. Has good experience as a CFO. Though cleanup is still needed, there have been good improvements in the business office's performance metrics since his return. Business office results seem to be the only metrics trending in the right direction currently. Seems organized and methodical. Is married with three daughters. The oldest two are in college while the youngest is a senior in high school. He is a proud Aggie and likes to be involved with his alma mater, where his oldest daughter attends. *Youngest daughter recently received an academic scholarship and graduates from high school soon and will be roommates with her older sister at his alma mater. Wife, Vanessa, is a successful real estate agent in the area. Very proud of his family.*

Rosie, VP of HR—the veteran in the group. Very self-confident. Has worked at Wisdom for more than twenty years in various positions. Is a wealth of knowledge about anything to do with the center and seems to be well known throughout it. Has been the only dependable and constant leadership person. Seems to have surprising loyalty to Wisdom despite its many challenges. Has four grown children and several grandchildren she loves to visit. Also likes to cook, and is an avid follower and fan of the local sports teams. She is also involved at the church she attends. Her faith is very important to her. *Cooking Mediterranean food is her favorite. Her oldest granddaughter, Rose, lives close by, and they have a close relationship. Loves the color orange.*

Sarah, VP of clinical services—experienced leader with good clinical knowledge and strong people skills. Likes to camp and go to the lake with her family. Has one son and one daughter. Her husband, Rick, is a high school science teacher. Grew up in a large family, many of whom live in the area. *Lives on the same street as her parents, and her mother has some health challenges. Her father, Donald, is a recently retired pharmacist. She is the oldest daughter in her family of seven siblings (three older brothers and one younger brother plus two younger sisters) and feels a great responsibility to watch over her parents.*

Grace was glad she was getting to know more and more about her team. She genuinely felt lucky to be working with such a great group of leaders. Though the numbers didn't show it yet, she felt certain they'd be able to accomplish some impressive things together.

We have one month to shine!

A Visit

Over the next few weeks, Grace continued to focus on creating clarity and establishing consistency. She also diligently performed her charity habits.

Arriving a little later to work than normal on a beautiful sunny morning, Grace was excited to see Dan already talking to her staff. She thought about going over to say hello but decided not to interrupt. Besides, she knew what he was up to and looked forward to his report.

A few days earlier, Grace had called Dan and asked if he would stop by the center. She wanted him to quiz her team members to see how effectively her consistent messaging around the building blocks and collective goals was going. She knew having an outsider's perspective would give her a good barometer on the amount of clarity she had created on these most important items. She was particularly interested to see how her leadership team would do since she felt she had repeated the message so often to them over many weeks now.

Around lunch time, Dan poked his head through Grace's office door and asked, "Do you have a minute?"

"Yes! I can't wait to hear what you have to share."

"Well, first of all, you shouldn't be discouraged," Dan continued. Grace felt a tinge of disappointment.

We must not be doing as well as I had hoped, Grace thought, and then said, "Uh-oh, that doesn't sound good."

"Now, wait a minute," Dan responded with a chuckle. "Let me explain."

"You better, and quick," Grace said, trying to relax and tease him but still feeling a bit worried.

"The progress you've made is actually incredible. For the most part, everyone at least had an idea of each of your building blocks and collective goals, which is a really good start.

"Some leaders and team members were on it one hundred percent while others struggled more. Only one of your department heads seemed sort of far off, but she stated she hadn't been here long. So the leadership team seems rather clear on what matters most." Dan paused for a second and smiled, adding, "Nice job."

Grace nodded and calmed down hearing the good news, but she knew more must be coming.

"There is more discrepancy among the floor staff, which is to be expected, and so many of them seem to be newer employees."

"Yes, we have done a lot of hiring since I arrived."

"I figured as much. Anyway, though some do know the basics of the building blocks and where to find the goals, a few were less sure."

Feeling disappointed, Grace wasn't certain how she should react as Dan continued.

"I will say that in most instances, however, once I shared your center's mission, vision, and values with them, most all of them seemed to instantly recognize them. Some even said they had heard them multiple times or had seen them one place or another, which is good. So nearly everyone seems familiar with them, which is fantastic."

Though she still felt a little discouraged that they hadn't completely aced it, she realized this was about what she had expected or maybe even a little better. After all, they had only recently begun to really focus on creating clarity and establishing consistency with the frontline staff and new hires a few weeks before.

"Overall, you've made excellent progress only having been here—what, three months now?"

"What? You don't know?" Grace said, now trying to give her former boss a hard time. "I thought you've been mournfully counting every day since I left. You mean to tell me that place over there isn't falling apart without me?"

Grace noticed Dan's cheeks turning red, and she laughed out loud. She decided she'd better let him off the hook and added, "Yes, about that, I think. I don't know anymore; it's all been such a whirlwind at this point. But yes, I think it has been about three months," she said with a smile.

"Well, the progress here is incredible in that amount of time, in my opinion. I'm quite blown away as I sit here thinking about it," Dan said with what seemed to be a look of approval. "Keep it up. Clarity and consistency are two of your best allies. And we do miss you." He grinned.

The two talked for another minute about clarity and consistency at Northfield during his early days. Grace enjoyed hearing more about his experience in turning that center around.

"The one thing about clarity is there's never a finish line. You must consistently repeat things over and over and over again until people start completing your sentences for you, like you used to." Dan said this with another smile. Only then will you know you're making real progress. But of course, that doesn't mean you stop repeating yourself."

Grace laughed within herself as she had not only sensed that Dan enjoyed it when she completed his sentences but also because she had heard Dan talk about the importance of repetition ironically over and over and over again. He also was a broken record when it came to talking about the mission, vision, values, goals, expectations, and standards at his health care center. The Northfield way of doing business was constantly rolling off his tongue and rang clear in everyone's ears over there. She recognized she had adopted many of his leadership behaviors and felt grateful again for his mentorship and support.

"This is the most important job you hold as the CEO," Dan went on. "To repeat yourself often about those things that matter most in order to create organizational clarity. I know I've told you this probably a hundred times." He trailed off. "Sorry about that."

"It's OK. You're being a perfect example of clarity and consistency with your messaging, and I need to hear it over and over and over and over again." Both colleagues laughed.

Grace was grateful Dan had taken time out of his busy schedule to come to her center. She decided she needed to take him out to lunch not only to say thank you but also to get his thoughts about more firmly establishing the other *C*'s.

"Gather your stuff; I'm treating you to lunch at your favorite spot today." And with that, the two colleagues were out the door.

Consistency

Lunch had proved to be a wise decision. Grace learned something from Dan about how he'd established the second *C* in the four *C*'s model that she hadn't ever heard before, although Dan had argued that fact.

In order to make absolutely certain he was consistent, Dan showed Grace what he called his daily, weekly, and monthly essential tasks list. He kept this list as a reminder of the things he had to do consistently to be successful in his role. He had claimed that without this cheat sheet, he'd be wildly inconsistent with many of the items on it. He asserted one reason was because they weren't all necessarily the most enjoyable parts of his job. Not all of them were things he looked forward to doing, but he knew they were vital. "And this is why consistency takes a lot of discipline," he had said.

At the end of the day, while reviewing Dan's copy of his daily, weekly, and monthly essential tasks list to build consistency, Grace began to create her own. After a little bit of time, this is what she came up with.

Daily					
Morning Huddle	☐	Key Metric Review	☐	Birthday Cards	☐
Labor Review	☐	Daily Rounds	☐	Customer Complaints	☐

Weekly					
Direct Report 1-on-1 Meetings	☐	AR Review	☐	AP Review	☐
Executive Team Meeting	☐	2-3 Staff Thank-you Notes	☐	Dept. Budget Review	☐
Marketing Meeting	☐	Applicant Interviews	☐	Open Positions Review	☐

Monthly					
Customer Satisfaction Results	☐	Financial Documents Review	☐	Monthly Key Metric Review	☐
All-Staff Meeting	☐	Update Goals Scorecard	☐	Contracts Review	☐
2-3 Thank-you Notes to Customers	☐	New Employee Orientation	☐	Strategic Partners Meeting	☐
Employee Safety Review	☐	Prepare Board Report	☐	Revenue Report	☐

She knew this list would need to be evaluated from time to time and even expanded. As she looked it over, she felt confident that she had been fairly consistent thus far with most of the important items she had put on the list.

Grace decided it would also be a great idea to encourage her leadership team to create similar lists for themselves in their individual roles. She felt doing this would help all of them develop good habits, perform well in their jobs, and establish consistency throughout the center.

* * *

During their next leadership meeting, Grace found herself sharing her list, talking about the importance of consistency, and encouraging everyone to make their own.

"Remember to include only critical tasks you should be doing daily, weekly, and monthly in order to have the most success and establish consistency within your roles, departments, and the center."

She also shared an experience she'd had working in a place where there had been a lot of inconsistency. "It got old listening to the leadership team say one thing but then do the exact opposite. And several times a new policy would be introduced only to be changed over and over again until everyone was completely confused about what the right way was." She hoped her example illustrated how inconsistency negatively affected everyone who worked there, herself included. Afterward, she thought she needed to share a more positive example.

"The consistent results produced at Northfield are a direct reflection of the consistency their team demonstrates day in and day out. If we can learn to be consistent, even with our daily, weekly, and monthly tasks, we can begin to see similar results. Consistency in the small things can produce big results. They can change the entire direction of our center."

All the leaders agreed to make their own daily, weekly, and monthly essential tasks list.

Grace wasn't finished, though. She had thought of another way that would help with clarity and consistency.

With the help of her team, Grace made a list of important meetings, including the days, times, locations, and who should attend. She also added to the list the primary objective of each meeting in order to make clear to everyone why it was important.

Though they had been quite consistent with holding these essential meetings, there was still an occasional question about a meeting time or location or who should attend. She believed creating this list and then distributing it would help with the first two *C*'s in the model.

Finally, Grace smiled as she found herself giving her leadership team a lecture similar to the one Dan often gave about consistency.

"We must each strive to be consistent with the things we can control, such as our actions, words, behaviors, and attitudes at work. And our approach to similar situations also needs to be consistent."

Most in the room were nodding.

She then added, "A high level of consistency from this group will produce feelings of security and trust among our team. People want to know they can count on us, and we can demonstrate that they can through our consistency."

Grace paused and wondered if anyone might have anything to add. Before she could even ask, Marshall jumped in.

"I can say from experience that no one likes to work for a boss who is all over the place with unpredictable ups and downs and highs and lows. I've been there before, and it is not fun."

"And our people need leaders who they can count on, in an environment where they know what to expect," Rosie added. "They need to know we will react the same way in similar situations and treat them the same way both in good times and bad."

"Very true. We will have good days and bad days, but the more consistent we can remain in how we handle stress, deal with difficult situations, manage change, or anything else that comes our way, the more security and sense of stability we will create for our team here at work. This will have a significant impact on our culture and results," Grace responded.

She noticed most of the team nodding in agreement, and she was grateful for their thoughts. Like Dan, she knew this was probably a speech she would give frequently as a reminder to help them always establish both clarity and consistency throughout their health care center.

More Consistency

Though Grace felt good about where the team was headed with consistency, she wanted to do more. Because she was operating under a short timeline, she knew she needed to be more diligent at establishing the four *C*'s model. With this on her mind, she had come up with something she believed would be helpful.

* * *

As her executive team gathered around the conference room table for their weekly meeting, Grace dove in.

"I know we spoke about consistency at last week's leadership meeting, and it's been nice seeing some of the daily, weekly, and monthly essential tasks lists you've developed. I applaud you for those. I have no doubt this will benefit our center as well as your effectiveness as leaders.

"Today, I'd like to continue the discussion on consistency. Specifically, I'd like us to focus on ways we can take a consistent approach to situations that come up here at work that may lend themselves to inconsistent responses, such as how we deal with separations of employment or how we react to sudden changes in the workplace."

Grace paused to see if anyone had a question or comment. After a moment she continued.

"Our approach to situations such as these where emotions can sometimes take over and get the best of us will be important for us in building consistency and strengthening our culture. So today, I'd like us to talk through some of these situations and proactively decide how we will handle them. Doing this now, and establishing a response without emotions in the moment, will help us have much better outcomes when they come up. So, the question we need to answer as a team is 'What will our consistent approach be to handling these situations as they arise?'"

Grace paused, thought for a moment, and then decided to ask, "Before we begin, let me ask: What is at risk if we don't decide now how we will approach these situations that can lead to an inconsistent response? Why does this matter?" She noticed her team seemed to be genuinely thinking through her question.

After a minute, Sarah finally said, "If we don't address these situations now, then our emotions may cause us to make rash decisions that aren't in the best interest of our center or our people. Or that aren't aligned with what we are trying to accomplish. So deciding now how we will handle these potentially volatile situations will help us be consistent in our response. We won't have to scramble and react in the moment. We'll be acting proactively."

"Great points," Grace said. "And if we can be consistent in our approach to these situations that are often handled inconsistently, we can really strengthen our culture here at Wisdom."

"This is interesting because just the other day, I was thinking about how one of our unit managers let a nurse go who had made a poor judgment in providing care to a patient. Though her termination was warranted, it wasn't handled well. The unit manager really let her have it on the floor in front of her peers and wasn't kind to her either as she escorted her out the door. It just wasn't the right way to approach it.

"I know many of our team members observed how she handled this termination, and it didn't communicate a good message. It was unprofessional and demeaning, and I wish our department could have an opportunity to do it all over again. I guess expectations of how we handle these things could have been more clear," Sarah shared.

"Great example. Had we decided beforehand how separations of employment were to be handled here at Wisdom each and every time, and then made it clear to all our leaders, this unit manager might have conducted herself very differently, in a much more positive way."

Finishing that thought, Grace noticed the silence in the conference room was palpable. She wasn't sure what everyone was thinking.

Finally, Marshall spoke up, breaking the silence. "But what that nurse who was terminated did was completely out of line. I think most of us would have done the same thing. Or at least something similar."

Though Grace appreciated Marshall's desire to show sympathy for the unit manager, she couldn't let his comment slide.

"I hope not, Marshall. I hope none of us would respond that way because it's not consistent with our values and mission. It's not consistent with how we want to do business here at Wisdom."

Grace let that sit for a moment.

"Yes, we all make mistakes from time to time and do things we regret, but we need to be better than this here. We need to consistently let people go in the same way, and we can always do it with respect, dignity, and kindness, no matter how upset we are."

"You mean with charity," Rosie suddenly blurted out.

"Yes, with charity." Grace smiled at Rosie, who was looking proud of herself. "This shouldn't have happened this way. But since we don't have a consistent and clear plan for how we approach the discharge of employment, essentially, any way we handle a termination will do."

The leaders again sat in silence for a moment before Grace added, "Let me share another example of why taking a similar approach is so important and how not having one leads to poor performance.

"Just the other day, I was complaining about the new health survey process, and I was doing it in front of many of you and others. I went on and on about how unfair it seemed and how it had the potential to really hurt our center."

"I remember that," Jenn said with a slight smile.

"Thanks, Jenn." Grace laughed. "Rather than taking a helpful and professional approach to the inevitable changes in our industry, all I've done is complain about them."

Grace allowed that to sink in for a moment.

"My response has not provided anything positive and has probably only hurt our team. It has brought us down. And this is exactly why it will be best to decide now as a team how we will consistently handle changes in the industry or in our workplace, or a separation of employment at our center. Doing this now will help us establish consistent responses together. And strengthening consistency will help us create a better culture which will lead to stronger results."

Grace then introduced the simple spreadsheet she had developed and named the "decide now tool." It wasn't fancy or impressive, yet she believed utilizing it could serve as a simple way to keep them aligned and reacting consistently. This is what the tool looked like.

Decide Now

Situation/Scenario	Plan/Approach

After Grace introduced the worksheet, the team came up with three scenarios they were certain would come up from time to time that often lent themselves to an inconsistent response. They then wrote out a plan for how they would approach each scenario in a consistent way. The three situations discussed were handling unexpected change, separating employment, and observing poor customer service.

After spending time together developing plans, this is what the team came up with.

Situation/Scenario	Plan/Approach
Handling Unexpected Changes	1. Stay positive. Look for the potential silver lining and good that can come from the change.
	2. Develop a plan (with input from the team when possible) to effectively implement the change and ensure success. (The plan should be centered around creating clarity, establishing consistency, adding celebration, and having charity).
	3. Share the upcoming change and the implementation plan with all who need to know.
	4. Create a way to evaluate the plan to make sure it is effective.
	5. Adjust the plan as needed (with input from team).
	6. Maintain and exhibit a belief that we will not only be ok but that we will thrive before, during, and after the change process.
Separation of Employment	1. Prepare employment separation documentation.
	2. Meet with the team member only when calm and when you have plenty of time to spend with them.
	3. Recognize you don't know everything going on in the person's life that may have contributed to poor performance.
	4. Always invite someone to join during the separation of employment discussion. Never do this alone.
	5. Review the separation documentation with the team member and inform them that their employment will be terminated.
	6. Give the team member a chance to share any thoughts, feelings, opinions, and actively listen to them. Don't judge, argue, or discredit comments.
	7. Share appreciation for what the person has done to contribute to the organization.
	8. If appropriate, offer advice and coaching on how to succeed in future employment opportunities and wish them the best of luck.
Team Member Providing Poor Customer Service	1. Stay calm and do not escalate the issue.
	2. If the team member is currently engaged with the customer, politely interrupt and invite the team member to speak with you in a private area (perhaps your office).
	3. Recognize you don't know everything surrounding the situation or what may be going on that might be contributing to the behavior.
	4. Meet with the team member and let them know what you observed was poor customer service. Allow them to share what they may feel is necessary. Reiterate our expectations of behavior with customers.
	5. Remind them that providing poor customer service is never allowed, is contrary to our mission and values, and is considered gross misconduct, which results in formal discipline and potential loss of employment.
	6. Based on the severity of the incident, inform them of the appropriate disciplinary action you will be taking (or inform them you will be speaking with their direct supervisor who will take the appropriate disciplinary action).
	7. Based on the severity of the poor customer service, invite the employee to return to work or ask them to take an extended break or go home for the day.
	8. As soon as possible, present the employee with the appropriate formal disciplinary action or termination.

161

Grace felt confident the decide now tool had done its job and would help her team be more consistent in areas in which they had struggled to establish consistency in the past. She and her team departed with plans to add to the worksheet in the future with more situations that invited inconsistent responses.

* * *

As fate would have it, a few days later, government officials announced major overhauls to the reimbursement system for health care providers. Though Grace heard about worries and concerns at most health care centers across Wiser Care, Inc., she and her team turned to the plan they had recently developed on their decide now tool for how they would approach such unexpected changes in the industry.

With a plan already in place for how they would approach the sudden change, Grace felt strangely calm about the impending changes, and so did her team. She knew Wisdom's team would handle the change just fine.

Employee Surveys

During Grace's second week on the job, she had asked her HR team to conduct an internal employee satisfaction survey to get a baseline of how the team members were feeling about working at Wisdom. It was no surprise to Grace, or really to anyone, when the results that came back were poor.

Sitting in their familiar places around the conference room table, Grace and her executive team were now engaged in a discussion about how to consistently measure employee satisfaction. They all agreed that if they were serious about their core value of "employee dedicated," then they needed to take greater care of their team members. They had come to the conclusion that in order to do that, they needed frequent feedback from them.

"OK," Grace now said, standing at the whiteboard. "To make sure we are clear on what we have decided, we all agree that we should conduct a quarterly satisfaction survey during the last payday at the end of each quarter, correct?"

Grace noticed all heads nodding. The team had determined that, at a minimum, these quarterly surveys would allow them to gauge how their people were feeling about working at the health care center.

"This means our next survey will be distributed at the end of this week. Do we think we can pull that off?"

"Absolutely," Rosie said with a smile, showing confidence it would be handled.

"Great," Grace said, adding, "and in conjunction with quarterly surveys, everyone feels good with the rest of our process once we tally the results?" She pointed to what she had written on the whiteboard.

**Wisdom HC's Team Member
Satisfaction Survey Plan**

1. Distribute surveys the last payday of each quarter.
2. Share results with the entire team at the next all-staff meeting following the survey.
3. Develop a plan to act on one or two feedback items based on results.
4. Share the plan with staff members at an all-staff meeting.
5. Provide updates on the plan and the progress being made to improve at each monthly all-staff meeting.

Again, heads were nodding around the room, and Marshall added, "I think this plan will be great."

"I agree. Consistently getting feedback and then improving on one or two items will definitely help us move toward becoming an employer of choice in town. I doubt any of our competitors are doing anything like this," Jenn now added.

"I've never seen this done before anywhere I've worked," Sarah chimed in, agreeing.

"Me, neither—not consistently like this," offered Bruce.

"This will be such a wonderful way for our team members to see we're serious about creating a great work environment for them. Consistently making small improvements to our employee experience will have a big influence on our culture; I know it," Rosie shared enthusiastically.

Grace also felt good about the plan, and she believed following it would help build consistency as well as have a positive impact on the other three *C*'s.

After putting their new employee satisfaction process through the four *C*'s test, the entire executive team agreed it was a system that would help enhance their culture and improve results.

* * *

Another week had passed, and the quarterly satisfaction survey results were in. Grace felt both excitement and apprehension as Rosie walked through her door to share the outcome of the survey.

"Well, are you ready?" Rosie asked with a smile.

"I think so. Are they bad?" Grace questioned.

"No, I don't think so. Let me show you."

After reviewing the survey results with Rosie, Grace simply felt tired. Though the results had improved significantly from where they were three months ago, Grace had hoped for an even bigger turnaround.

What stood out during the review of the survey responses were that first, her staff felt the mission of their organization was important. This was great news. And second, regrettably, the staff did not feel they were getting enough recognition at work for doing a good job.

There was evidence throughout the survey results that clarity and even consistency were improving, but Grace realized celebration was lacking. It was clear to her that the time to really start focusing more on the third step in the model, the third *C*, had come. *It's time for more celebration.*

By the end of the day, Grace felt a strange sense of both exhaustion and exhilaration. She decided this was in part because she was both inspired and unsatisfied by the employee satisfaction results.

On top of these feelings, probably more than anything else, Grace felt more hope than she could remember for improvements and continued better days.

Come the following Monday, Grace knew exactly what the topic of discussion would be with her executive team. But before Monday came, she would receive some welcome news.

Part Three

Celebration and Charity

Welcome News

It happened! After three and a half months, it had finally happened. A part of Grace could scarcely believe it, but on the other hand, she had known it would only be a matter of time.

While looking at the monthly financial reports, Grace realized that not only had Wisdom ended their consecutive streak of months in the red, but the profit turned for the month was stronger than even Grace had anticipated.

This is how Wisdom's net income chart looked for June.

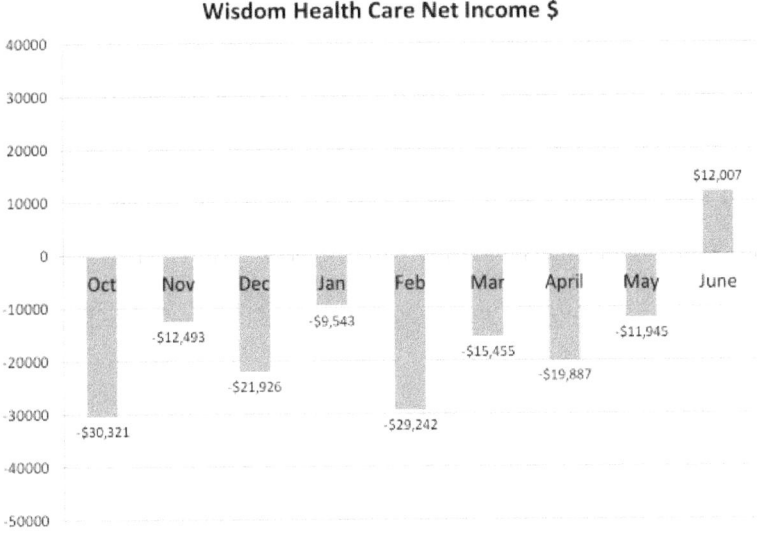

Wisdom Health Care Net Income $

Grace felt for a split second like she was on top of the world. She knew Wisdom needed this. *Yes, yes, yes! Finally, tangible results to show for all our efforts that people outside these four walls can see.*

After a moment of celebration, Grace brought herself back to reality. She knew one month's positive results were only a small step in what needed to happen at Wisdom to save it from being sold. She knew they still had a long way to go.

As she reviewed the financial statements, it was easy to see revenue was up, and costs were down. What wouldn't be evident in the numbers to those outside the health care center was the fact that her focus on implementing the four *C*'s model and establishing charity, clarity, and consistency was finally paying off.

As she leaned back in her chair, she began to contemplate some of the bigger problems that still existed.

For one, tension was mounting between Sarah and Marshall. Each had valid concerns about the other's performance and the handling of recent issues, yet each wanted the other person to conform to their way of thinking. And the crux of the problem was that the quality of care at the center was still not where it needed to be and not progressing as quickly as they all wanted it to.

Another problem was that, though revenue had grown and the VP of marketing had hit the ground running, things were already slowing back down again.

Worst of all, Wisdom might still go up for sale. Grace knew that one good month might not be enough for Tom and the board.

So to pretend things were now all wonderful or that the health care center was humming along smoothly after three and a half months of intense focus on the model would be a big stretch. Yet, despite these ongoing problems, Wisdom had come a long way from where it was not too long ago.

Though far from where she hoped Wisdom would one day be, Grace was grateful to see the progress.

I only hope June's results will slow down the board's eagerness to sell.

* * *

As Grace reviewed the key metrics with her entire leadership team, she was quite impressed again with what she saw and how much they had improved in some key areas. She offered plenty of congratulatory comments to her team, and she could see they were thrilled.

"This is a huge step in the right direction. I couldn't be more proud of this team and how far we've come in a short amount of time. If there's anything I've learned over the last three and a half months here at Wisdom, it's that we can conquer anything. Any challenge we face, any obstacle that comes our way, any setback we may encounter, I have no doubt we can do this.

"As we continue to commit to living our values and mission, I know in time we can achieve our vision. Yes, we still have a long way to go to reach our goals, but I know we can get there."

Grace noticed heads nodding and lots of smiles. As she took one final look around the room at the team, she observed what she felt was genuine happiness but also looks of exhaustion. She was keenly aware that most on her team had been putting in long hours alongside her to get the center to this point. She felt a bit of regret for not doing more celebrating sooner.

My team has done a lot. It's time to bring celebration into full focus.

Unexpected Visitors

"The health inspectors are here," Grace heard her receptionist say somewhat frantically over her office phone intercom. Her heart sank.

With a major overhaul of clinical systems currently underway and having so many new clinical team members, including Sarah, Grace worried her center wasn't prepared and thus susceptible to negative findings.

"These visitors certainly weren't expected today, now, were they?" Sarah said to Grace under her breath as they both headed to the conference room to meet the surveyors.

"We can do this," Grace whispered back quickly.

Sarah smiled. "I agree. We've got this."

Though Grace wanted to continue to exude confidence, she knew the center needed a bit of a miracle to come out of the inspection unscathed. And it wasn't because Wisdom's patients were in imminent danger or even that they weren't receiving appropriate care. Rather, it was how tedious the inspection process could be. If policies and procedures and rules and regulations were not followed with exactness, then they would get dinged. And she knew how a poor outcome from this survey could really hurt their progress and momentum.

After meeting with the health inspectors and explaining the transition of clinical leadership and the changes being made at the health care center, Grace and Sarah began to rally their team. Though it was something they strived for each day, they desperately needed every team member doing their best work today.

Thankfully, everyone seemed to respond quickly and with confidence. Grace prayed things would turn out well.

As the surveyors walked around the center observing care, talking to staff and patients, and reviewing document-tation, Grace grew nervous. Even a single citation might influence Tom and the board of directors' decision to sell. And based on surveys at Wisdom in the past, she had little hope that the inspectors wouldn't cite at least some negative findings. *I wish I had a magic wand to instantly make everything better, but unfortunately, things don't improve with a snap of the fingers*, Grace thought.

On the outside, Grace did her best to exhibit faith that they'd do well, and she was constantly encouraging her team. On the inside, she was stressing out about the potential ramifications the results of this unexpected survey could have on the future of the health care center. She knew the findings of the surveyors could literally change everything for Wisdom.

* * *

After several hours of surveying and inspection, the moment of truth had arrived. Grace felt her hands sweating as she and Sarah sat across from the inspectors to debrief.

"I'd like to say there are plenty of opportunities for improvement here," started the first health surveyor. "Your medical records are unorganized, your patients have some complaints, and nursing documentation appears sloppy in several places."

Grace's heart sank. She wished she had had more time to prepare. After all, she had only been at the center for four months.

Now not only was Grace worrying about the sale of the center, but she also fretted about how a poor outcome on the survey might hurt their already-fragile reputation as well as how it might bring back the dark cloud she had felt hovering over the center when she first arrived.

"With that being said," the surveyor continued, "the complaints we heard were minor, and plenty of staff, patients, and even family members shared with us they are seeing improvements each day."

"Many even shared they'd gotten to know you two and think you will continue to make things better here. I'm actually surprised you've gained so much support in such a short amount of time. Many seemed to personally know the new CEO and VP of clinical services."

Whether on purpose or not, Grace felt the second surveyor said this with a hint of cynicism.

"From my vantage point, though disorganized, you're meeting the minimum requirements and regulations."

Grace held her breath.

"So there will be no deficiencies cited at this time."

It took Grace a moment to compute what had just happened, and then suddenly, she had the urge to jump out of her seat and hug the surveyor. Instead, she offered a smile and said, "Thank you. We're committed to making this a health care center everyone can be proud of."

"I hope so," responded the first surveyor as she stood. "Heaven knows, based on some of the inspections here in the past, this place could use it."

Grace wasn't sure how to respond to that comment but decided it didn't matter. Somehow, they had done it.

As Grace stood, she felt a huge sense of relief wash over her. She was so grateful to Sarah, who had carried a heavy load ever since starting at Wisdom. She had performed wonderfully, and without her, Grace was certain things would have turned out much differently. The last thing Wisdom needed right now was bad news.

She also felt so much gratitude for Dan and the four C's model. Without them, she was certain her charity habits, which seemed to have influenced the results, would never have taken place.

Once the surveyors had left the center, Grace invited her team to come to the conference room. As everyone crammed in, she let them know about the good news. Many on the team let out a collective sigh of relief, and a few even cheered.

Now that the worry was over, Grace believed the unexpected fire drill had been a positive event for her team. She was certain the good result would boost the team's confidence and help them see they were headed in the right direction.

* * *

Later that evening as she sat in her office reflecting on her day, Grace suddenly felt more gratitude for the four C's model. She was convinced her efforts around charity, clarity, and consistency had helped the inspection earlier in the day go well.

Looking over the model on her desk, she suddenly thought, *We have to celebrate!*

A Celebration

As employees arrived to work the next day, they were greeted with the delightful smell of freshly cooked waffles and a large spread of toppings. They also were handed a few raffle tickets and were told to hang on to them until the announcement of winners was made later in the day.

In the afternoon, Grace called out the winning tickets for the raffle prizes. She also thanked her team for all their work and recognized the outstanding results on the survey. To add a little more fun, she then called up three willing volunteers to participate in a dance-off for the final prize.

All in all, it was a fun way to celebrate their recent accomplishment. And Grace knew this celebration was only the beginning of many more to come.

Thoughts on Celebration

"Celebration is more than just having fun, although that is certainly a big part of it," Grace said to her executive team. "Celebration is also about tracking or measuring progress toward goals, and it's about recognition.

"I'm not sure I've done a good enough job with this—recognizing all the progress we've made. This is our next step to fortify and build a strong culture. We need to focus on this third *C* in the model. It's time to celebrate more at Wisdom."

Grace paused for a moment, and everyone seemed to be listening closely.

"So how do we start helping our people feel more and more that their efforts are recognized and appreciated? And how do we make Wisdom a more enjoyable place to work?" Grace asked her team.

For the next hour and a half, the executive team discussed what they could do at Wisdom to better establish celebration through measuring progress, recognizing team members more, and having more fun. Though they came up with a lot of really good ideas, there were a handful they settled on.

First was the mission award. This would be given each month to the employee who best exemplified living the mission day in and day out. The award included a framed picture of the team member along with a short story about how they specifically had lived their mission of creating excellent experiences for each person they served.

These mission awards would then be displayed in a prominent location in their center.

Next was the Wisdom values award. Similar to the mission award, it would be given to someone who exemplified a specific value. The recipient would receive a small gift, and a specific example of their demonstrating the value would be shared in the monthly health care center newsletter as well as at the monthly all-staff meeting.

Grace loved these two individual awards; however, the one she liked best was the one they had created last.

Even though she had been hesitant when the idea was first brought up because of their current financial situation, she once again had been persuaded by her team to reconsider. She was grateful they were sharing their thoughts and pushing back on her opinions. After some debate surrounding the idea, Grace came around to seeing how the program would be a wise investment. In fact, it now seemed obvious.

During their discussion, Spencer questioned why they didn't tie some sort of celebration to the number of collective goals they hit each month from their scoreboard. From there, the idea grew until they decided that the number of goals reached each month would determine the type of celebration they'd have. The more goals hit, the bigger the reward and celebration for the month.

The team determined that on most occasions, these celebrations and the distribution of awards would happen during the established monthly all-staff meeting. This would provide the best opportunity for the entire team to celebrate together and be recognized. It would also fit perfectly with Grace's already-consistent presentation of the month's performance and her update on the goals during the meeting. She had come to realize this program would further highlight the importance of what she was already sharing.

Grace also loved the fact that this program would provide recognition to all team members while reinforcing the collective goals they had established as a group. To her, team awards were better than individual ones.

The program would also allow them to have some fun together each month.

The executive team determined that the program would pay for itself in increased engagement, productivity, and teamwork. Perhaps most importantly, it passed the four C's test.

Because budgets were still tight and financial woes were still looming, the executive team knew they had to be careful how they designed the celebrations each month. In the end, this is what their new celebration program looked like.

Wisdom Health Care Center
Team Performance Celebrations

Goals Reached	Celebration
1	Popcorn Party
2	Ice Cream Party
3	Waffle Party
4	Pizza Party
5	BBQ Party
6	Wisdom Health Care Center Logoed Cooler
7	Hawaiian Luau Party
8	Wisdom Health Care Center T-Shirt
9	Wisdom Health Care Center Camping Chair
10	Team Member and Family Carnival (food, games, prizes)
11	Wisdom Health Care Center Fleece Jacket
12	$25 Gift Card
How It Works	
Each month we will see how many goals we accomplish. Based on the number of goals we reach, we will do the corresponding celebration above to recognize good performance and have fun together. These celebrations normally will take place at our monthly all-staff meeting so please come!! This will not be our only celebration, but will be one that provides a fun way to recognize our progress, work together, live our mission, and reach our goals.	

As their meeting concluded, Grace was excited to introduce this program to her broader leadership team as well as to her entire workforce at the next all-staff meeting. She felt this type of celebration program, along with the other ideas they had come up with to celebrate, were really going to add to the culture they were cultivating through their focus on the four C's.

180

Loyalty

It was Friday night, and Grace was out to dinner with her family, a luxury she hadn't been able to enjoy very often since she started at Wisdom. It felt good having a meal with her husband and children at one of their favorite restaurants near their home. And though she tried to forget about work and really enjoy this time with them, the reality was Wisdom was never far from her thoughts.

At the end of the meal, her husband exclaimed, "Look at that; our next meal here is free." The family had been dedicated patrons over the years and were part of the loyal customer club at the restaurant.

"That's great news," Grace said with a smile and then their youngest squealed excitedly.

"Does that mean we can eat here again tomorrow, Mommy?"

Grace and her husband laughed.

"You are too cute with that adorable smile that I love so much," Grace responded. "But why don't I make my world-famous homemade pizza tomorrow night for dinner, and we can come back here sometime soon."

"Yay!" her daughters cheered in unison.

* * *

As the family headed home after an enjoyable evening out, celebration was back on Grace's mind. *If there are customer loyalty programs out there that encourage us to*

181

keep coming back, why not create a team member loyalty program? she thought quietly.

After some more thinking, Grace had in her mind what she felt would be an effective employee loyalty program that would recognize and reward staff for their dedication to Wisdom and add celebration. She was sure it would be another way to help them retain staff and reinforce their core value of being employee dedicated. Grace was excited to share her ideas with her executive team on Monday.

Loyalty Program

As Grace ran through the proposed team member loyalty program with her executive team, everyone seemed to agree it sounded like another great way to add celebration.

After some iterations and tweaking, they felt they had created something that would further add celebration to their center. The Wisdom loyalty program included recognition along with special awards and perks based on tenure.

"This program clearly communicates that we value our team members. It will be another great way we can create an exceptional work experience for them," Rosie said.

"I love that we're recognizing and rewarding team members who stick with us, especially in front of their peers. Turnover in our industry is so high, it only makes sense to reward them for sticking around," Sarah now added.

Rosie was then asked to tie up any loose ends and pull it all together before they introduced it at the next all-staff meeting. All agreed it would help their center increase celebration and live their mission and values.

"Wait, we didn't officially put it to the four *C*'s test yet," Marshall jumped in just as everyone was about to leave.

"You're right," Grace said. Though it would have been easier just to allow everyone to walk away at this point, she wanted to make sure they were staying consistent to the process they had agreed on. They had committed to putting all new programs, systems, and decisions they made through the four C's test before implementing them.

"Can I head out real quick? I'm sure you've got this, and I need to jump on a call that's starting soon," Jenn queried.

Again, Grace knew the easy answer was to let her go, but consistency rang in her brain. "We made a commitment as a team to put all our decisions to the test, and your input is important, Jenn. We should remain consistent with this. It won't take us long."

Though Grace could tell others were eager to go as well, everyone sat back down, and they ran through the test. Going through the exercise, each executive team member felt it would help them establish not only celebration but also clarity, consistency, and even charity. They didn't find any ways in which it might hinder their ability to establish any of the C's. And it was aligned with their mission and values.

"It passes with flying colors," Grace said. "Thank you, everyone, for sticking around for a few extra minutes to go through that. It's important we remain as consistent as we possibly can be, and it's also important we continue to focus on the four C's model. Thanks for catching us on that, Marshall."

Though one or two of her team members seemed mildly annoyed in the moment, Grace was certain she had done the right thing. She felt great about each of the recognition programs they had come up with to add celebration.

Enormous Letdown

As good as the last month's numbers had been, they were completely forgotten when the financial documents for July came out. Wisdom's results in Grace's fourth complete month as CEO were similar to the results in her second month, May, which were not good.

Though Grace knew the center had struggled during the month with customer volume and revenue, she couldn't believe the bottom line for the month was almost back to where it was when she started.

This is what the net income graph looked like.

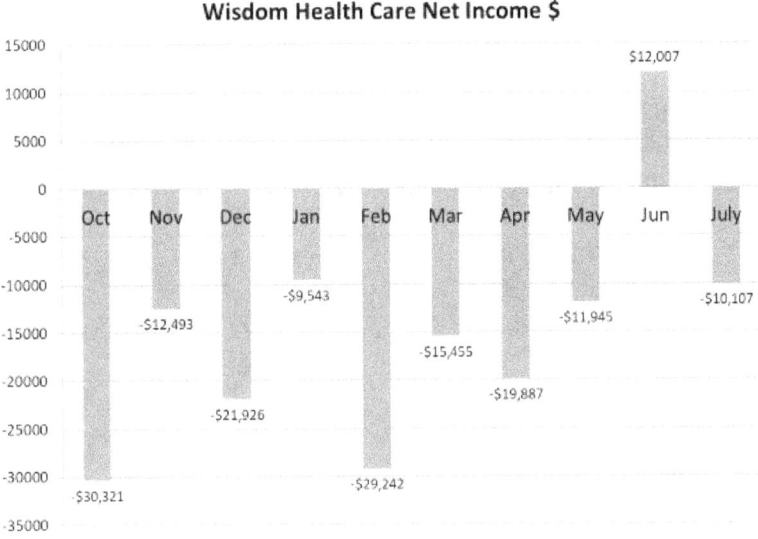

After combing through the numbers, Grace knew she needed to talk to Dan. She wanted his perspective and thoughts. She picked up her office phone, feeling deflated and discouraged.

* * *

Calling Dan proved to be helpful. During their phone conversation, Dan reminded Grace about all the positive things that were happening and that she was building Wisdom for a sustained, long-term turnaround and not just a flash-in-the-pan type of result.

"These things take time," Dan reassured her. "You got everyone's attention with last month's strong results, and this month is still better than most of those before you arrived. All this shows signs of a real turnaround there at Wisdom."

Dan had pulled up the financial reports during the conversation, and they had gone through them together. Though the actual numbers were disappointing, Dan pointed out that many of the leading indicators were on a strong positive trend: customer satisfaction, clinical outcomes, cash collections, and employee turnover. He also shared his center's financials for the month and pointed out that it had been a really slow month in terms of volume for everyone in the area.

"You know, it isn't unusual for things to slow down come summertime."

As Grace hung up the phone with Dan, she wanted to be more determined than ever to succeed, but in the moment, she couldn't shake her disappointment.

Attempting to pick herself up and forget about the net income numbers, Grace saw the powerful effect her emphasis on the four C's model was having in most areas of the center.

Even though the bottom line was still not where she wanted it to be, the reality was that contract workers had been completely eliminated, customer complaints were decreasing, employee satisfaction was on the rise, costs were now being managed and decreasing, and relationships in the community were improving. Grace had a lot of positive things to point to, and her team had made a lot of progress. Though she felt awful inside, if she were completely impartial, the difference between where the center had been when she began and where it was today was undeniable. And no one who was familiar with Wisdom could dispute it.

Grace concluded she wouldn't let the bottom-line results of July detract her or her team from pushing forward and continuing to establish the four *C*'s.

Feeling Worse

As bad as Grace had felt when analyzing the monthly results of her health care center on her own and with Dan, she now felt worse as she reviewed the results with her leadership team. She had seen how hard they had worked and saw the disappointment in many of their faces. She knew they were dwelling on the negative numbers a lot more than the positive ones, just as she had.

Before redirecting their attention, she realized she was grateful for their reaction. It showed they were invested in their results and wanted to do better. This attitude seemed to her like a stark contrast from where they had been only four and a half months ago when she had arrived. She knew their expectations for themselves had grown.

With everyone looking dejected by the end of her review, Grace went back and emphasized many of the positive things that came from July's numbers. She pointed out the good progress in many important areas and made sure to celebrate each win by offering congratulatory comments to her team.

Although she could tell it still stung that not all numbers had improved, the mood in the room had become better, and she believed most left the meeting with a new determination to keep pushing toward their goals.

* * *

Later that week, as the entire team gathered for the monthly all-staff meeting, Grace was happy to present the first celebration based on the number of goals they had achieved in July.

Since they had only reached two goals, the celebration was less than what Grace was hoping for, but it was recognition that would not have happened prior to the development and implementation of the new program.

Grace enjoyed the ice cream party during the all-staff meeting and felt most of her team did as well. And after spending time with her team, Grace wanted to reward them with even more next month. She knew how hard they were working, and several impressed her by asking what they could do to help the center reach more goals. She was grateful so many were committed to doing better.

Grace was convinced she would be able to do more for them in the coming months.

After her review of the monthly performance and goals during the meeting, Grace sensed a growing resolve among the entire group to improve performance.

Rollout

The introduction and subsequent rollout of the employee loyalty program seemed like a hit. The handful of long-tenured team members seemed to genuinely appreciate the recognition they received as they were grandfathered into the program and praised for their loyalty to the health care center. And Kaylee, the exhausted nurse Grace had met during her first official round, ran over and gave her a big hug.

Grace could feel celebration improving throughout the center and honestly believed it was more fun to be at Wisdom than she could ever remember. If momentum continued around the four *C*'s model, she was certain good results would follow.

Suddenly, she felt her phone vibrate and saw it was Tom.

She dreaded answering it, but she put the phone to her ear and said casually, "Hello, there. How are you, Tom?"

"I'm doing good, Grace. How about yourself?"

"Oh, still just slaying dragons and living the dream here at Wisdom."

"Listen," Tom said, seeming as if he was ready to cut to the chase. "We're going to be sending in some reinforcements to help you and to review the operation. Though June was a big success, July didn't seem to turn out as well as we were all hoping. I think this person can help you."

Though it was common practice for Wiser Care, Inc. to send in support from the corporate headquarters to help struggling operations, to her knowledge, Wisdom had received a lot of such help over the years without much to show for it. Grace didn't like the sound of this, and she questioned Tom's motives.

In the end, however, Grace realized she wasn't in any position to turn away the help. So rather than share her displeasure with the idea, she said, "OK, sounds good. I'll be happy to work with whoever you'd like to send to help us." She then added, "And by the way, July will be the last month Wisdom loses money. I know it isn't evident yet, but the fly wheel is starting to spin here, and I'm confident August's results will be better than June's."

"You're really that certain?" Tom asked, sounding doubtful.

"I am," Grace responded as confidently as she could.

"OK, Grace. Well, Peter will be there Monday." And with that, the two hung up.

Peter

A week later, Peter was sitting across from Grace in her office explaining he had just returned from vacation and apologizing for taking so long to show up. Grace shared that she wasn't worried about it and was happy to have any help he could provide. She also asked Peter about his experience at Wisdom.

"I've been sent here many times over the years," he responded. "This is a tough place. From what I've observed, it's always been hard to find good staff and keep leadership around. This makes everything just that much more challenging, you know."

Grace nodded, and Peter continued.

"For example, I've helped implement many processes over the years, but nothing ever sticks. And the main reason, from what I can tell, is the constant turnover in staff." Peter then sat back for a moment and said, "I hope you're here to stay; this place needs stability and dependable leadership."

Grace assured Peter she was there to stay and then shared with him what they had been doing. She even introduced him to the four *C*'s model, explaining it was something they had lived by at Northfield.

Appearing genuinely curious, Peter asked a lot of questions about it. So, besides just talking about the model and how it worked, Grace also shared some specific things they had done or were doing at Wisdom to reinforce clarity, consistency, celebration, and charity. Peter seemed impressed but also skeptical.

After the lengthy conversation about the four *C*'s model, Peter finally changed the topic and shared a few things he planned to work on, and Grace gave him a few small tasks as well. She wondered if he'd actually be much help.

* * *

After four days of working at the center, Peter seemed genuinely impressed. "Things are really different here. I'm blown away."

Grace was happy to hear this and interested in knowing more about his perceptions. "What do you think has changed?"

"I'm not sure exactly," Peter said before adding, "but you've found some really good staff. They seem to be doing really well."

"I agree. I've been fortunate. Our team is great."

"I just hope they stick around," Peter commented.

"I think they will. This is the best place to work."

Peter shrugged his shoulders as if he wasn't sure how to respond and then shared some small concerns with the medical records processes and some dietary services issues. While he offered to assist with improving these few areas identified as opportunities, Grace believed he had already helped more than he realized. Peter's unbiased opinion about how the center was doing meant everything to her. She then had an idea.

"I do have one other thing you could help me with."

"Sure, what is it?"

"Would you mind sharing what you shared with me about the improvements you've noticed at our leadership huddle tomorrow morning? I think they'd love to hear an outsider's perspective, especially from someone who has been familiar with the center over the years.

"Sure, I'd be happy to."

* * *

When Peter shared his honest opinion with the entire leadership team the next morning about how amazed he was with the progress at Wisdom, hearing it again and seeing the faces of her team made Grace's day. She believed it was a moment she wouldn't soon forget. And although she hated to admit it, she was extremely grateful Tom had sent Peter to help after all.

Growing Results

August had passed like a whirlwind, and the financial numbers for Wisdom were about to come out. Based on all indications, Grace knew it was shaping up to be a good month, and she wasn't shocked when August proved to be the strongest month Wisdom had seen in over two years, nearly doubling June's performance.

This is how the net income graph looked.

Though Grace was glad Tom and others at Wiser Care, Inc. would see the positive results, she was more excited to share them with her team.

As they gathered for their monthly financial review, Grace could see the anticipation in the eyes of many of her leadership team members. As she went through the numbers, their delight grew and grew as she pointed out how the center had improved in nearly all areas. Grace offered plenty of compliments and congratulatory remarks and celebrated their success.

Finally, when Grace shared that their net income was the best the center had seen in over two years, a few in the room clapped while others cheered.

Grace was elated to see the progress and to share it with her team.

* * *

A few days later came the really fun part—at least, it was fun for Grace, mostly because she had gotten to know her frontline team so well. At the monthly all-staff meeting, she announced they'd reached six goals and shared what the celebration would be as a result of their accomplishments.

Handing out personalized Wisdom Health Care Center logoed coolers to everyone for having reached six goals in the month was a joy. Grace wondered if the worst was behind them and hoped the monthly celebrations would only continue to grow.

Grace then made it a point to share how proud she was of her team and let them know she believed it was only the beginning.

"As we continue to work toward our goals, and as each of us strives to live our values and mission each day—to create exceptional experiences for each person we come in contact with—this will be only the beginning of something much bigger. Each of you is playing an important role in contributing to something meaningful. We are going to have a significant impact on our industry, and others will look to us as an example of excellence."

Later that evening, Grace sat quietly at her desk, reflecting on her day. She thought about how much things had changed and the momentum that was building. It had been only five and a half months since her arrival in early March, yet Wisdom already felt like a much different place. She knew her own and her team's incessant focus on the four C's was working.

Goodbyes

"Peter isn't coming back to your center," Tom was saying to Grace now over the phone.

"Oh, why not?" Grace was surprised. He hadn't even completed the task he was working on, at least not to her knowledge.

"Well, for one thing, he told me he was bored and didn't feel he had much to do there at this point, other than a few simple things in medical records. He says things seem to be running surprisingly well, far better than he's ever seen over there."

Tom then paused before saying, "I'll tell you, Grace, he's really impressed. He wanted me to encourage you to keep doing what you're doing. He also mentioned something about Northfield and an implementation of some kind of leadership model. Anyway, it seems to be working."

Grace laughed to herself as she listened. Peter had been surprised by how much the center had improved.

"Well, I'm sorry to see him go so fast, and I apologize that he felt bored here. I can assure you there's still a lot of work to be done to reach our goals. But I'm sure there are other centers that are struggling more than we are right now." Grace said this with a bit of self-satisfaction.

What she hoped now more than anything was that the thoughts of selling the center would be wiped completely off the Wiser Care, Inc. radar.

Tom quickly added, "It's quite amazing what's happening there. Well done."

Grace couldn't resist. "So is the timeline for selling the building on hold at this point?" She held her breath, hoping that perhaps this was the real reason Tom had called.

He hesitated, and then it sounded to Grace like he was fumbling with his phone.

"Sorry about that, I almost lost my phone there. And actually, that's the other reason why Peter isn't coming back. The board approved the sale of Wisdom Health Care Center a few days ago. I'm sorry to inform you, but the decision was made, and the deal is already with the broker. I'm truly sorry, Grace."

Grace literally had to catch her breath as what Tom had just shared completely caught her off guard. It felt like he had just kicked her in the stomach all over again. After a long moment recovering, she said with disbelief, "How can this be, and why didn't you tell me sooner? What can we do to make sure Wiser Care doesn't go through with this and sell Wisdom to a competitor? I can assure you, it will be a huge mistake."

"I'm sorry. You knew the timeline we were under, and besides, Wisdom has been a black eye on the organization for many years now. Selling it is really what makes the most sense for the future of our company. And you've done a lot to make it a more attractive asset. Your recent performance has increased the asking price. For that, I couldn't be more grateful."

If Grace had had the ability to reach through the phone and smack Tom, she would have. She tried to cool down and not allow her intense emotions get the best of her.

"And be assured I've already secured a new CEO position for you. Our leader at the Lakeland Health Care Center will be stepping down, and I've already received approval to have you placed there. You won't even have to go through the normal internal interview process. You'll be able to transition right over when it's time. And the move will be a fairly close one for your family."

Grace thought for a moment, then gathered her words carefully. "I'm not leaving Wisdom, Tom. I can't. And I won't." She paused for a moment. "I want to be part of the acquisition. I'll stay on with the new owner if they'll allow me to. I want to be part of the deal."

"What? Are you serious? Come on, Grace," Tom replied, sounding baffled. "Lakeland is a beautiful health care center with a much stronger reputation and performance history than Wisdom. It will be a breeze for you there, and you'll love—"

Grace interrupted him midsentence. "I'm serious, Tom. I'm not leaving Wisdom. I want to stay on with this team. You can consider this my resignation from Wiser Care."

Grace hoped Tom understood she was serious, but he made another feeble effort to persuade her.

"Grace, you know these transitions to new owners are hard, and CEOs who stay on board with the new company rarely last longer than six months. I'd really hate for them to use you to stabilize the transition and then spit you out."

The irony of Tom's words couldn't have been more poignant. Grace wanted to offer a stinging remark but decided her best course of action would be to end the call.

"I'm serious, Tom, I plan to stay at Wisdom. Thanks for the news. Goodbye."

Response

After taking some time to calm down and process the shocking news she had just received, Grace called her trusted mentor, Dan.

"You're kidding me!"

Dan was just as stunned as Grace was about Wisdom already being listed for sale.

"Let me give Tom a call. I'll also call Sandy."

Sandy was Wiser Care, Inc.'s CEO, whom Dan knew well.

Grace was thankful he was willing to try to help, though she wasn't sure it would do much to reverse their decision. She also asked if Dan felt there was more she could do to pull back the train that apparently had already left the station.

He encouraged Grace to send an email to Tom and Sandy detailing Wisdom's plan for continued sustained improvement in performance while highlighting all they had already accomplished in six months. Though still angry and bewildered, Grace thought it was a good idea, and just after midnight, she hit send on a lengthy email that she hoped would somehow change what evidently had already been decided.

Grace hadn't told Dan what she had said about leaving Wiser Care, Inc. to remain as the CEO at Wisdom. She worried that he would react negatively, and she didn't want him to try and talk her out of it. She did, however, reaffirm her desire to stay on with the new owner in her email message to Tom and Sandy. She wasn't sure if it would help or hurt her cause. More than anything, Grace hoped Wiser Care, Inc. would reconsider their choice and retain ownership of Wisdom.

* * *

As Grace finally dozed off early in the morning, she imagined how her team would react to the news of being sold. After observing their reaction to Wisdom's most recent performance results, there was no doubt in her mind they'd be shocked and devastated too. She hoped that day would never come.

Charity Effect

It was the beginning of a new week, and Grace was struggling to overcome the anger and frustration she was feeling inside knowing Wisdom had been put up for sale.

"Hey, boss, are you OK? You haven't seemed quite like yourself the last few days," Rosie said as Grace walked out her office door to do her morning round.

Grace knew she had to pull herself together and maintain a more positive demeanor. She needed to continue to build Wisdom's culture through the four *C*'s model. *I need to control what I can control*, she thought before saying, "Yes, I'm fine. I just really want things to turn out well here."

"We all do." Rosie smiled, adding, "I've been here a long time, and it's never felt like this before. Everyone is so . . ."—Rosie hesitated for a moment as if to find the right word—". . . excited. You're doing a great job and we all owe you. Especially me."

Grace smiled. "I think you're being too kind, and really, I owe you more. For sticking it out and supporting me, especially after such a rough start."

"I've seen worse."

The two colleagues laughed.

"You've never given up on this place, Rosie. I wish more people out there were as committed to Wisdom as you are."

Fearing she might divulge more about the fate of the health care center, Grace hurried off down the hall. As she turned down hall two, she saw one of her favorite team members, Mary Ann, at the far end.

Mary Ann was an experienced certified nursing assistant who had worked one of the busiest halls in the entire health care center for nearly a year now. Grace liked to describe her as a hardworking team player, and no matter how crazy things got on her busy hall, she always had a great attitude. And the level of compassion she had for those she provided care to each day was always evident. *She's about as good as they come*, Grace thought as she smiled, waved, and continued down the hall toward her.

Grace then recalled the story Mary Ann had shared with her several months ago.

Asked why she had decided to join Wisdom, Mary Ann had stated that for one, it happened to be the closest health care center to her home, and two, she'd had a bad experience working with a competitor down the road.

Surprised and curious to understand more, Grace had pried.

Mary Ann then revealed that her young adult son had run into some legal trouble, which caused her to miss some work unexpectedly. Though she had always been diligent with her attendance prior to this, her supervisor over at the competition wasn't happy she was missing work. After she requested a day off on short notice again to help her troubled son, her supervisor had given her an ultimatum—either she came to work as scheduled or she'd be fired.

Mary Ann had told Grace she'd felt completely torn. She wasn't about to abandon her son, but she didn't want to give up the place where she had built her career over the last fifteen years. Though it had somehow worked out and she had kept her job while missing work that day, the damage had been done.

Mary Ann had no longer trusted her employer after the incident, and this bad experience forever affected the way she felt about working there. Soon after, she made the decision to quit and applied for a position at Wisdom.

In Grace's mind, Mary Ann's story was a classic example of a lack of charity. Fortunately for Wisdom, Mary Ann had landed there and had been a top-notch performer from her very first day.

"Good morning, Grace."

"Good morning, Mary Ann. Your hall is looking great like always. How is your morning going?"

After some small talk, Mary Ann shared something that caught Grace completely off guard. "You know my old employer has been calling me a lot lately. They want me to come back."

"Oh," said Grace, trying to hide her astonishment.

"Yes, they must really be desperate over there because they've offered me a lot more money than I was making before I left."

Grace was now beginning to feel worried. Though she didn't know for sure, she assumed that Mary Ann, as a newer employee, was being paid less at Wisdom than she had been when she left the other place after fifteen years of service. Grace was certain the offer must be more than what she was currently earning and began to think about what she could say or do to convince Mary Ann to stay at Wisdom.

"Of course, it would be more than what I'm making here," Mary Ann said, confirming Grace's fears. "I did think about it for a minute, but then I came back to my senses and told them no way. There's a lot more to work than money."

Grace felt sudden relief. What Mary Ann said next, though, surprised her even more.

"I've been doing this kind of work for nearly thirty years, and I've never had a CEO say hi to me in the morning like you. That's something money can't buy, you know. Even if it does get crazy around here sometimes, it's nice knowing someone cares."

Hearing how an act so small could mean so much astounded Grace.

"We're so lucky to have you here, Mary Ann. Thank you for all you do to make Wisdom a special place."

Both ladies smiled, and after some more light conversation, Grace walked away, realizing the tremendous effect her simple charity habits were having on her people. She then reflected on how her charity habits were affecting her personally as well. After all, she had just resigned from Wiser Care, Inc., a company she had grown to love, to stick with a team she had learned to love even more.

Mary Ann is sacrificing to stay here and make this a better place, and Rosie has too—and so will I, Grace thought as she completed her morning round.

Sandy

The next day, Grace received a nice phone call from Sandy, the CEO of Wiser Care, Inc., about the email she had sent to her and Tom a few days ago. Sandy seemed truly interested in learning more about what she had shared in her message.

During the conversation, Sandy mostly just listened. She also apologized for not speaking to Grace before the deal was pushed out the door and said it was a mistake not talking with her first. Though Grace appreciated the call, Sandy never mentioned that the health care center would be taken off the market. For this reason, Grace wasn't feeling very hopeful.

After replaying the conversation several times in her mind, Grace concluded that trying to decipher Sandy's words and getting her hopes up were probably not the best use of her time and energy. She had done what she could. *The only thing I can do now is continue to improve things here*, she thought.

Rather than worrying more about the pending sale, Grace turned her attention back to the four *C*'s model. She knew that if her team continued to improve clarity, consistency, celebration, and charity, they'd all be part of an unbelievable turnaround story. She even believed September's net income results might be just as good as August's numbers. She would soon discover she was wrong.

Another Month

"That is more than a thirty percent increase over last month!" Bruce exclaimed as Grace shared the net income numbers with her executive team.

"This is really good progress," Marshall added.

"It's almost hard to believe we're still at Wisdom, right?" Jenn pronounced excitedly.

Another month's financial performance had come out, and Grace could tell everyone in the room was elated by what they saw. Everyone, that is, except for her. Though she knew she should be ecstatic, the pending sale dampened her spirits.

"Can we just let that graph linger up there for a while and not take it down?" Rosie said, laughing.

This is how the month's net income graph looked.

Wisdom Health Care Net Income $

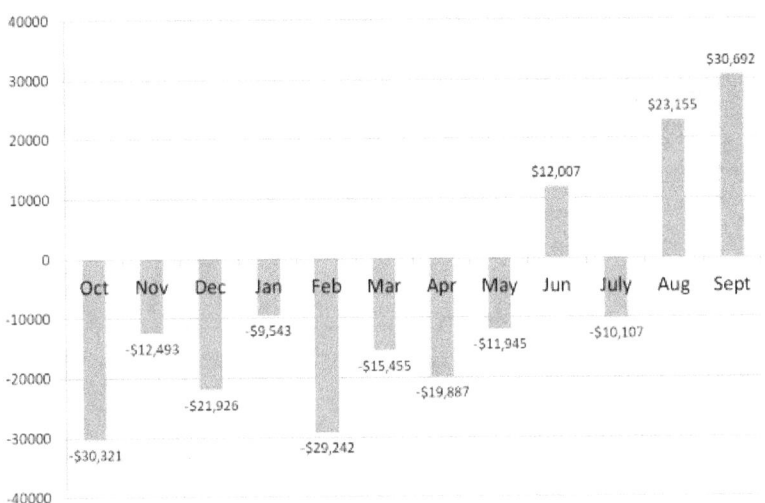

To Grace's knowledge, August and September were the best back-to-back months Wisdom had had in more than four years.

Later that day, as Grace reviewed the monthly results and celebrated with her entire leadership team, she couldn't help but wonder what the latest news was on the sale. She felt, now more than ever before, that Wiser Care, Inc. was making a big mistake. She wondered if she needed to do something more than she already had to try and prevent it from happening.

* * *

"Congratulations on another fantastic month," Dan said over the phone. "I'm so excited for you and the team. They must be thrilled."

"Have you heard any news on the sale?" Grace asked, cutting off his enthusiasm. She wanted to enjoy the results, but she just wasn't in the mood.

"I haven't heard anything new, have you?"

"No."

"Do you think positive months at Wisdom are here to stay?" Dan asked. "Two in a row is something probably most didn't expect to happen, especially so fast. Of course, it doesn't surprise me."

Grace was slightly amused by Dan's question. She felt that, out of everyone, he would be the least surprised by the trajectory they were on at Wisdom. After all, he was always preaching that the four *C*'s model would lead to these kinds of results.

"I don't see any reason we'd ever have a losing month again at Wisdom. The momentum is real here, and this is why I'm so upset the center is still for sale. I'm having a hard time enjoying our results right now." Grace knew she was unloading a little bit on Dan, but she felt she had no other outlet.

"Wisdom has been losing money for a long time. However, with two months of profitability and three in the last four, this has to catch people's attention. You've done great work over there. You need to celebrate."

After some more conversation and congratulatory remarks from Dan, Grace hung up her phone. She wanted to feel good about the center's progress and performance, but it was difficult.

She then contemplated calling Tom but hesitated, not wanting to hear bad news. *What if he tells me Wisdom has already been sold?*

After a few more minutes of consideration, she decided she had no choice. She had to know.

"Hello, Grace," Tom said, answering the phone. "I was just going to call you. Well done."

"Well done?" Grace questioned, momentarily confused.

"Yes, congratulations on having the best month's net income results at Wisdom in more than four years."

Grace wanted to say something sarcastic to rub it in a little bit but instead said, "I'd really just like to know where you're at with the sale and if you or anyone over there has reconsidered."

"I don't have any news for you. But like I told you, as soon as I know anything, I'll make sure and let you know."

"So no interested buyers yet?" Grace asked, trying to get as much information as possible. She wondered if maybe no one was interested because of Wisdom's reputation and long history of poor performance. She worried her month's good performance would actually hurt her cause and propel the sale forward. *Am I inadvertently attracting more buyers by improving performance?* was the next question she wanted to ask Tom, but she didn't dare.

"No serious buyers yet to my knowledge," Tom answered. "Most suitors see Wisdom as a distressed asset when they review the financial and clinical outcomes over the last few years."

Grace began to fret that her fears of aiding the sale might actually be true.

"Is it time to reconsider then?" Grace asked bluntly.

Grace noticed Tom hesitating before he said, "Maybe it would be wise to reconsider, but turning back now isn't that easy. There would be a lot of ramifications, and the board was firm on their decision." Tom hesitated again before adding, "This isn't something they take lightly, and a lot of thought and consideration went into the decision. They'd been discussing it for years—long before your arrival."

Grace heard him sigh before stating, "Honestly, I can't ever remember a time when they've turned back on a big decision like this one. Once a decision is made, it's made. I'm sorry."

Grace felt defeated all over again and thought Tom was done speaking. She was about to end the call when he finally added, "But I'll bring it up at our next board meeting in a few weeks."

After a moment of silence, he added, "By all accounts, it looks like you had a stellar month. Two in a row, in fact. I'm proud of you. Congratulations."

Three in a Row

We did it again! Grace thought as she opened the latest month-end financial reports. *The fruit of our concentrated efforts on the four C's model is paying off.*

Wisdom Health Care Center now boasted three positive-net-income months in a row with a steady trend upward. Grace was thrilled, and so was her team when she shared the net income graph with them.

This is how it looked.

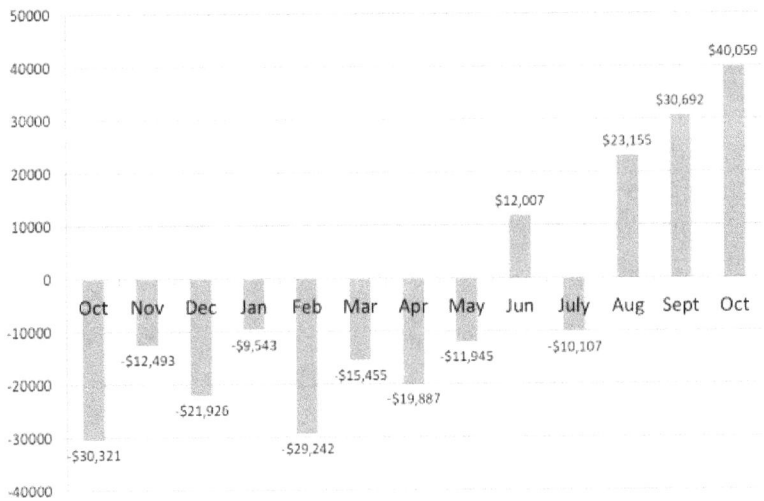

Wisdom Health Care Net Income $

As Grace reviewed the mission, vision, and values and then shared their updated progress on goals during the monthly all-staff meeting, everyone seemed ecstatic. They had hit seven goals, which was a new record, and it was time to celebrate.

As the department leaders served ham, pineapple, and poi at their luau celebration, Grace noticed a lot of happy faces. It was such a contrast to what she had observed when she had first arrived.

She recognized focusing on the four C's model had almost done the impossible for Wisdom, which was now beginning to make a name for itself. Even many of the Wiser Care, Inc. corporate officers were taking notice as several of them had sent congratulatory emails to Grace on the positive trends at the center. "It is really hard to remember the last time Wisdom had three consecutive months of growth. Well done, Grace!" Sandy had written in a message to her.

Grace and her executive team celebrated their recent results over lunch at a nice restaurant. And though significant headway had been made, their conversation quickly turned to their goal of winning the Industry Excellence Award.

"We've made some real progress," Marshall stated.

"In only a few months," Sarah added.

"But if you look at our results in comparison to where we need to be for the Industry Excellence Award, we still have a long way to go," Bruce reminded everyone.

"That's true, but based on our current trajectory, I'd say it's coming more and more into sight. If we continue on this path, it won't be too long before we start to get there," Jenn shared.

"And to think, only a few months ago, some of us around this table had the wild idea of setting our sights on the Industry Excellence Award," Grace said with a smile.

"I must admit it seemed completely crazy at the time, but things are changing."

"I'd say in large part because of everyone's laser focus and commitment to the four C's," Marshall commented.

"Creating clarity, establishing consistency, adding celebration, and raising the levels of charity within our center has been a game changer for us," Bruce agreed.

"So let's talk more seriously about the Industry Excellence Award now," Rosie said, jumping in, also sounding excited.

"I don't see any reason we can't make a real run for it next year. We'll have a few more months to ramp up, and then we can hit the ground running. What do you think?" Marshall said, looking at Grace.

Grace hesitated for a moment as the pending sale of the center made her think twice before saying, "I completely agree."

The rest of the lunch felt electric as the group enthusiastically discussed how they could get to where they needed to be to qualify for the award.

During the discussion, Grace kept steering them back to the four C's model and how they, as the executive team, could continue to establish each C to accelerate their results. After all, in seven and a half months, things had significantly improved at Wisdom because of their relentless pursuit of instituting them.

"What if we spend each of our next four executive team meetings discussing each C in the model again and then decide one thing we can do to further establish that C in our center?" Jenn asked.

"I think that's a great idea," Grace said, and all agreed.

Though Grace had loved lunch with her team and their conversation during it, in the back of her mind, she fretted how working under new ownership might derail their momentum and goals. And she despised the thought of how it might adversely affect some of them on the team. New owners often had their own opinions on certain leadership positions and often brought in some of their own people.

A lot has changed at Wisdom, but how different will it be in another seven months? Grace thought, worried.

Only time would tell.

Charity Focus

It was Monday morning, and Grace and her executive team were once again surrounding the conference room table. Their discussion for the day was charity. Grace reviewed how charity worked in the model, explaining once again how it was a magnifier.

"For this reason, it encircles the other three *C*'s," she said. "Remember, charity is helping people feel they are known and cared about at work. We can take any action with or without charity. And when high levels of charity exist, they will have a multiplying effect on our efforts around the other three *C*'s. For this reason, I thought this *C* would be the best place to start as we look again at each element of the model over the next few meetings."

All heads around the room were nodding.

After brainstorming several ideas for how they could raise levels of charity within their organization, the team concluded that helping new employees feel cared about and known as quickly as possible was one of their biggest opportunities. Though they were improving, Wisdom was still losing more new hires than they wanted to admit.

Together, the team decided on a more robust new employee welcome program. It would include the creation and installment of a new team member welcome board, which would display pictures and information about newly hired staff; a welcome letter from the CEO, which would be accompanied by their Wisdom name badge; and presenting new hires with a few Wisdom Health Care

Center logoed gifts, delivered by an assigned leadership team member from a different department on their first day. Though Grace felt it was about time to wrap things up, Bruce surprised her with his next comment.

"Is this really good enough? I mean, it will help with charity, yes, but is it sufficient?"

"What do you have in mind, Bruce?"

"I'm not sure. It just feels like something is missing."

"I agree." Rosie now jumped in. "This is a good start, but perhaps we can do more."

The team discussed this for a few more minutes, unsure of what to add until Bruce interrupted the conversation.

"I think I've got it. All this stuff is nice, but if a new hire's interaction with their colleagues is poor, I'm unsure this will help as much as we need it to."

"I'm not sure I understand what you mean," Rosie now said.

"What I mean is we can shower our new people with gifts and do nice things for them, but if the person who's training them or the coworkers who work closest to them aren't kind and respectful—in other words, don't show charity—will our plan help all that much?"

Grace decided it was time to jump back in.

"I think these simple actions will help more than we realize, but Bruce brings up a great point. We ought to do more to help them feel the Wisdom love from their coworkers from the beginning and not just love from the leadership team."

"What if we trained the trainer?" Rosie said.

"I like that idea, Rosie; tell me more," Grace replied.

"What if anyone who will be asked to train someone goes through a training we create to help them do the job with more charity, clarity, and consistency?"

"And celebration too," Spencer added.
"Complimenting them or giving them a high five when

they do something right or just recognizing their effort can mean a lot to someone new who may be struggling to adjust to a different way of doing things."

"I like this idea," Sarah said.

"What if we ask new hires to complete a little survey after their initial few days with us to get feedback on their experience? And in this survey, we can include specific questions about their trainer as well as their interactions with their coworkers," Marshall suggested.

"I like that idea too," Sarah commented again.

"This would help us know what individuals are doing a good job training and maybe which ones aren't cut out for this responsibility," Rosie added.

"I think we could even provide a Wisdom Health Care 'charity training' at our next all-staff meeting and talk about the importance of welcoming and getting to know new team members on their units," Jenn now said.

"If we can add these elements to what we've already discussed, our new hire experience is really going to go through the roof," Bruce commented.

Grace was impressed with what Bruce had pointed out. The four *C*'s model had changed the way he was thinking about things, and she believed it made him an even more capable leader and contributor.

"This is perfectly aligned with our core value of being employee dedicated. What a great way to show we're serious about this value," Spencer stated.

"I think we're really onto something now," Grace offered, feeling a sense of pride in her team. She was grateful for what she felt was the honor of leading them.

After some more discussion about the details and assigning tasks that needed to be completed before the rollout, the executive team felt confident the program would successfully help new hires feel they belonged and were part of the Wisdom family right away.

The team then put the new program through the four *C*'s test, and it passed. Next, they set a goal of completing all the action items and solidifying the details so they could roll it out by the beginning of next month.

As they left the meeting, all agreed it was a positive step toward helping them establish more charity throughout their entire health care center.

Monday Clarity

"How can we continue to improve clarity?" Grace asked her team the following Monday. Though she had some thoughts, Grace wanted to first give her team a chance to share what they might have in mind.

After a few feeble ideas were offered that no one seemed to have strong feelings about, Grace decided to provide her thoughts.

"During my rounds recently, I've had some team members ask me about our evaluation process. Many aren't sure what it looks like and if or when they might receive one. I've also fielded plenty of questions about annual pay increases. Additionally, in analyzing our most recent employee satisfaction scores, one of our lowest marks is on the question about receiving adequate feedback on performance at work.

"Based on all this, I think we need to increase clarity around our employee evaluation process. Specifically, I believe it's important we try to make crystal clear how often we plan to present formal feedback to our team members, as well as the specific criteria we will be using in our formal evaluations."

"This sounds like a great idea to me," stated Rosie, and all the others seemed to agree.

"I thought it was clear we don't do raises or give evaluations and feedback here. I mean, I've been here for nearly three years now and have never seen one," Jenn joked.

Though everyone in the room laughed at her sarcastic remark, Grace realized it might be a bigger problem than she had thought.

"I know formal feedback and evaluations are important to our people. Making this process widely known throughout our organization will help us improve our culture. Does this sound like a good place to focus our efforts today to increase clarity?"

After Jenn's comment, Grace was convinced this was where they needed to concentrate their efforts, but she wanted to ensure others felt the same way.

With heads nodding around the room, Grace said, "Perfect. Let's focus the remainder of our meeting on improving clarity by eliminating ambiguity and uncertainty around our employee evaluation process.

As the discussion went on, the executive group debated the best possible evaluation process for the center moving forward. After an hour and a half of good input, idea sharing, brainstorming, and deliberation, Grace felt it was time to wrap up the meeting for the day.

"Let's allow Rosie to synthesize everyone's ideas and put them into a more formal plan, and then perhaps we can meet later in the week to review. Does that sound OK to you, Rosie?"

"Absolutely," Rosie said, and then before ending the meeting, they all agreed to meet again late Thursday afternoon to continue their discussion and finalize their decisions.

* * *

It was now Thursday, and the team picked up quickly where they had left off on Monday. After Rosie explained what she had put together, there were some questions asked, opinions shared, and refinements made to the process. In time, the team came away with what they believed to be the best decision for their revamped formal employee evaluation process. They also developed a plan for how they'd communicate the updated process to the entire team and make sure it was clear even as new people joined the organization.

"OK, I think we have a pretty good plan here. Let's put this to the test. We need to make sure this evaluation process will help our culture and not hurt it."

"I don't see any way this will hurt our culture," Marshall said.

"I agree," chimed in Rosie.

Knowing everyone was probably ready to leave, Grace thought about pushing the test aside. She hesitated for a moment, remembering the second *C* in the model.

"I agree it seems to be a no-brainer," Grace offered, adding, "but I think it would be wise if we put it to the test. Besides, we committed to being consistent at putting our decisions through the test, and I don't think we should abandon this practice now. It won't take us long."

"I agree we should stick with it," Sarah said.

"Obviously, we all feel this new evaluation process will help us with clarity. How about any of the other *C*'s?" Grace now asked.

"I think it gives us an opportunity to celebrate and share our appreciation with our team," Sarah offered, and all seemed to agree.

"It also has some potential to raise levels of charity, in my opinion. I mean, it won't do anything to hurt it, and it will give us another opportunity to get to know our team members better through this formal feedback program," Jenn added.

"OK, so it certainly passes the first question of the four *C*'s test." Grace then asked the second question. "Will it impede our ability to establish or to reinforce any of the *C*'s? I guess the only one we really haven't talked about yet is consistency."

Surprisingly, everyone sat quietly after the question was asked. Grace sensed there was some hesitation.

Sarah finally said, "I'm a little worried about that one. I mean, the program sounds great, but implementing it consistently may prove to be difficult. I worry about my team's ability to consistently pull it off."

"I'd have to agree," replied Jenn. "With all the people we are requiring to be involved in this process, I can see a lot of potential bottlenecks."

"And some leaders will be more diligent with following through with this process than others, which means some of our employees may get consistent feedback while others may not," Bruce said.

To this, Rosie commented, "That wouldn't be good."

"And what about when we have a leadership vacancy? Who is going to pick up the slack and make sure employees in that department receive their eval?" Marshall said.

"I know what you're thinking over there, Bruce, but it won't be me," Marshall said, chuckling as Bruce eyed him, then smiled.

After some more discussion, the team realized that, though the evaluation process could really add clarity, it also presented a real threat to consistency. After a little more discussion, they concluded they had no choice but to tweak the system they had already spent a lot of time developing.

"I know we've spent a lot of time on this already, but if we try to roll it out the way it is, I think we all agree it will hurt our culture rather than help it. It doesn't pass the second question of the four *C*'s test," Grace said. She sensed some disappointment, and she was a little frustrated herself. "I know it isn't ideal to have to rework this, but we can't compromise one of the four *C*'s. If we do, it will make life harder for us in the future."

Everyone agreed. And although it was getting late in the day, the team decided the best time to work it out was now.

After some more discussion and reworking of what they had originally created, the team finalized what they felt would help establish each of the *C*'s, or at least wouldn't hurt their ability to improve the levels of any of them, and would be a good process for feedback. It now passed the four *C*'s test.

"We'll have Rosie finalize the details, and then we'll introduce the new evaluation process to our team," Grace said. Though everyone looked tired, she could tell they were satisfied with what had taken place and the decisions they had made together.

"Thank you, everyone, for staying much longer than expected and helping iron out this important process. I think it will really help us improve clarity and even reinforce the other *C*'s in the model. Good job, everyone."

As the leaders said their goodbyes and left the conference room, Grace was grateful she had stuck with the second *C* and had put the new employee evaluation program to the test. She knew if she had failed to do it, it would have been a misstep and would have hurt their culture.

* * *

As was often the case, during the executive meeting, Grace had received several text messages. As she was scrolling through them sitting at the desk in her office, she noticed one from Tom. She quickly looked to see what he had typed, hoping it wasn't bad news.

It simply read, "No news to share at this point. Just wanted to keep you up to date."

Grace fumed inside, realizing Wiser Care, Inc. had obviously not changed its mind.

She thought about the best way to respond, but in the end, she decided it was best to just let it be. "OK" is all she sent back, and she headed to her car at the end of another successful day.

I hope the new owner of Wisdom will be a good one.

Consistency Meeting

The topic of discussion at the next week's Monday executive meeting was consistency. With the holidays fast approaching, the conversation turned to establishing consistent annual traditions and celebrating with their team in a consistent way over the holidays. Grace liked the idea and knew if her center could create some fun and memorable holiday traditions, they would provide something her team could count on and look forward to at the end of each year.

Together, the executive team decided on some meaningful and fun traditions, such as sponsoring a few employees in need by surprising them with food baskets and gifts, as well as having an annual leadership team white elephant gift exchange in which the funniest or most unusual gift would get an award. Both were simple ideas but could add to their culture.

What was most exciting to Grace about their plans to establish consistency was that she could see how many of them would reinforce not only consistency but also celebration; charity; and even, in some ways, clarity. The team put their new Wisdom holiday tradition ideas through the four C's test, and each passed.

At the end of the meeting, all the executive team members seemed to leave feeling confident their plans would help improve the culture at the health care center.

As the team departed, Grace's mind wandered. She began to worry how new ownership might alter the decisions her team was making. Would she continue to have the flexibility Wiser Care, Inc. provided her as the leader of her health care center? Would they recognize the progress they've made and encourage them to keep going? Or would they even be interested in keeping her and the other executives around?

At any moment now, all our plans and momentum could come to an abrupt stop.

She prayed the new company acquiring Wisdom would allow her and her team to continue down the path they were on.

Celebration Monday

"Based on all we've discussed thus far, I think our biggest opportunity to add more celebration in our center is to consider how we can celebrate daily," Grace said to her team. "We've gotten better at adding bigger celebrations, but the reality is, like the other three *C*'s, we should be striving to increase celebration on a daily basis."

"On a daily basis?" Bruce questioned Grace.

"Yes. Each day is an opportunity to further establish celebration."

"I'm not sure I understand. Are you talking about throwing some kind of party every day then?" Bruce again asked, looking genuinely perplexed.

"No, I'm not saying we need to throw a party every day. I'm talking about more simple things, like telling someone 'Good job' rather than just walking by and not acknowledging it or stopping to give someone a high five when you notice they took great care of a patient."

"What about congratulating someone in our daily morning huddle for completing a project or something?" Rosie offered.

"That's a great one," Grace responded. "Stopping to celebrate our team members can really mean a lot to them and add to our culture. Too many good things go unnoticed, but it doesn't have to be that way here at our health care center. Does anyone have other ideas of a simple celebration that we could do often?"

"How about writing a thank-you note to someone who really stepped up to help a coworker out?" Sarah said.

"Even telling people 'Thank you' seems like a way to celebrate them to me," Jenn added.

"Those are both good," Grace replied. "Imagine if each of us consistently did at least three or four of these celebrations each day. That would mean about twenty-five people being recognized a day and well over a hundred in a week."

"That sounds pretty amazing," Marshall said.

"It does," Bruce agreed.

"Such simple ways to increase celebration in our health care center," remarked Spencer.

"And to improve our culture," added Sarah.

"And to represent our core values," Jenn said.

"And to help us live our mission and achieve our vision," Bruce said, now looking at Grace with a big smile as if he was giving her a hard time.

"I think you all are finally getting it." Grace paused for a moment, adding, "And to think Tom told me I should really be worried about this group of leaders when I first arrived."

Everyone in the room froze for a minute and then laughed.

After more discussion of daily celebrations, the team came away with a list of how they could apply the idea of celebrating each day. This is what the list looked like.

```
┌─────────────────────────────────────────────┐
│         Wisdom HC's Daily Celebrations        │
│                                               │
│  1.  High five or fist bump someone you       │
│      observe doing a great job.               │
│  2.  Offer a sincere compliment to someone    │
│      working hard or going above and beyond   │
│      the call of duty.                        │
│  3.  Write a thank-you note, card, or email of│
│      appreciation.                            │
│  4.  Recognize someone by telling others      │
│      around them about how they are adding    │
│      value and contributing.                  │
│  5.  Catch someone doing something right and  │
│      say "Thank you."                         │
│  6.  Send a congratulatory or appreciative text│
│      message to a team member.                │
│  7.  Leave a small token of appreciation in   │
│      someone's work area.                     │
│  8.  Publicly acknowledge someone for doing a │
│      good job in a meeting, such as during our│
│      daily huddle or even on a conference call.│
│  9.  Invite someone to your office and simply │
│      tell them, "Thank you," "I appreciate you,"│
│      or "Good job."                           │
│  10. Hand out small tokens of appreciation to │
│      people you catch doing good work.        │
│                                               │
└─────────────────────────────────────────────┘
```

By the end of the meeting, all members of the executive team had committed to looking for opportunities to do at least three of the items on the daily celebration list each day. Grace was convinced if each of them did it, it would really help improve celebration and strengthen their culture.

Then she had an idea: "Before we go, what if we had a little more fun with this?" Grace enjoyed the curious looks she saw on most of their faces. "Let's each keep a tally of our small acts of celebration each day over the next two weeks."

"OK," "Sure," and similar responses came from everyone in the room.

"And there may be a little celebration in store for the executive who has done the most," Grace added.

Everyone seemed to enjoy that idea.

After a quick run through the four *C*'s test, it was clear to everyone these daily celebrations in no way would hinder their ability to establish any of the *C*'s and would strengthen several of them.

As Grace walked out of the conference room at the conclusion of the meeting, her phone began vibrating in her pocket. Looking at the screen to see who was calling, she felt her heart sink. It was Tom.

"Hello," Grace answered flatly. Though she wanted to stay positive, she was certain this was the call she had been dreading.

"Hi, Grace. I need you to do something for me," Tom responded coolly.

Grace had learned over the last several months that when Tom had something on his mind, he didn't bother much with chitchat.

"If you're not doing it already, I need you to find a chair and sit down."

Based on Tom's voice, Grace had a sick feeling in her stomach. *The center has been sold.* She could feel her heart racing and her blood beginning to boil. *How could they go through with it?*

Trying to maintain her composure, she responded, "Look, just say what you have to say, OK?"

"Well . . ."

Grace heard him hesitate and could hardly handle it that he was taking so long to spit it out. *It's not a total shock at this point; just say it*, Grace thought.

"Wiser Care has decided to retain the Wisdom Health Care Center. It's no longer on the market for sale."

"What?" Grace said softly, almost to herself, as she felt her knees buckling and quickly searched for a chair to sit down in.

"That's right, Grace. Wisdom is no longer for sale."

Grace still couldn't believe it. She had been certain his call meant everything was about to change for her and the team.

"It was officially taken off the market as of this weekend. This has never been done before in the history of our organization."

"I'm not sure what that means," Grace commented, still in shock.

"In the past, when assets have gone up for sale, we've always stuck to the plan. You've done something truly remarkable there, and people recognize that. For the first time in a long time, there's hope Wisdom might become a profitable asset in our portfolio of health care centers."

Grace was full of emotions, but mostly, she was elated. She wanted to shout for joy, and then suddenly, she felt unexpected tears welling up in her eyes.

"Thank you" was all she was able to say.

"I'm sorry. I know we put you through a lot," Tom said, sincerely now. "It seemed like the right thing to do, but the way you've begun to turn things around over there—well, it's garnered a lot of attention.

"To be fair, this doesn't mean Wiser Care will never reconsider the decision in the future, but for now, all plans for the pending sale of the center are out the door. And I have a feeling, based on the path you seem to be on, that it won't be much of a concern for you anytime soon."

Grace could hardly believe it. Her team had done it! Somehow, they had done something that had never been done before in the company's history.

"Oh, and final numbers for November's performance were just sent out a minute ago. I think you might want to take a look at them. All of us are in shock. I really should be thanking you."

The two talked for another moment, and then Grace hung up the phone. She felt an enormous sense of relief wash over her.

A few moments later, she opened her laptop to look at her financial reports for November. She immediately scrolled to the net income graph, and this is how it looked.

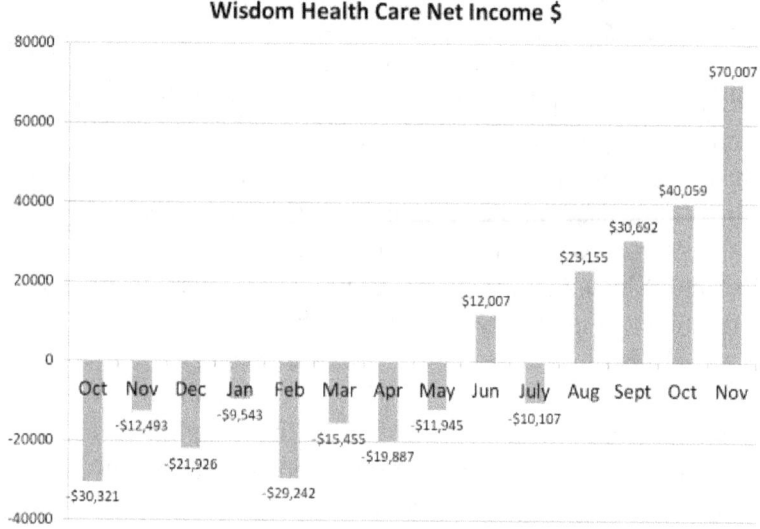

Grace momentarily allowed her emotions to get the best of her as tears ran down her cheeks. The tough days; sleepless nights; and feelings of doubt, anger, and fatigue had paid off. *Wow, we've done it. It's a miracle!* was about all she could think at that moment.

* * *

It was now 3 p.m., and Grace had called an emergency executive team meeting. As everyone gathered in the conference room, she noticed some concerned looks on a few faces.

"What's going on, Grace?" Sarah finally asked, knowing that was the question on everyone's mind. Grace finally pulled the tablecloth off the stack of items covered in the middle of the conference room table, revealing a pile of wrapped gifts. Grace handed one to each person in the room, and the question "What is all this about?" was asked repeatedly.

Once everyone had a gift, Grace allowed everyone to open them at the same time. Inside was a framed picture of their executive team. It was a photo taken at their celebratory lunch meeting just over a month ago, where they had spent most of their time talking about the Industry Excellence Award. She also included a personal thank-you note written to each of them.

Though Grace told everyone the celebration was about achieving the best financial month in Wisdom's history under Wiser Care, Inc.'s ownership, the reality was that it was about so much more than that.

The relief and excitement Grace felt about being able to continue with her team was indescribable.

The Cherry on Top

It had now been almost exactly twenty-four months since Grace had started as CEO at Wisdom Health Care Center, and things couldn't be more different from when she arrived. Though the center did not continue with a perfect trend upward—there were certainly some highs and lows—Wisdom had developed into a consistent high performer in all aspects of their business. Now, because of her team's relentless focus on the four *C*'s, there was a real outside chance the once-deplorable Wisdom Health Care Center would qualify for the prestigious Industry Excellence Award.

Grace recalled how absurd the notion had seemed when a few members of her executive team had brought it up nearly two years before. A lot had happened since then. Grace hoped they could somehow pull off what would be viewed by most as a miracle.

"I can't believe this is really happening," Sarah said to Grace as they headed toward the exit at Wisdom. "I've never been a finalist before."

"And I've never attended the actual award ceremony."

Both smiled.

"You better have plenty of battery life on that phone," Marshall yelled down the hall after them.

"I promise I do. I'll keep streaming until the winners are announced."

"And we'll all be huddled here around the screen, watching in anticipation," Rosie said, waving.

The awards ceremony was a bigger and longer event than either Grace or Sarah had expected.

"Why does the excellence award have to be last?" Sarah whispered.

Grace could tell that, like her, Sarah was both nervous and excited.

"Remember, just being a finalist is a big deal. We can be proud of that alone."

"I know, but I want to win."

Grace smiled at her colleague.

* * *

The industry association leader had already called out two winners for the Industry Excellence Award, and neither had been Wisdom. Grace felt certain their chances of winning this year had vanished, but she felt good to be in attendance surrounded by many of the best in the field.

"I think we should have won," Sarah said to Grace, looking a little disappointed as the announcements continued on the stage.

"And our last excellence award goes to . . ."

Grace held her breath.

". . . Wisdom Health Care Center."

Grace turned to Sarah with incredible disbelief, and then the two hugged and cried and hugged again with voices screaming from the speaker on Grace's phone as the team celebrated back at the center.

The C's have helped us accomplish things beyond my wildest dreams, Grace thought, accepting the award in front of the audience with tears forming at the corners of her eyes.

The Model

An Overview of the Model

Too many leaders and organizations fail to produce desired results because they neglect to place emphasis on the important elements contained in the four C's model. Though Grace used certain strategies to establish clarity, consistency, celebration, and charity in her health care center, there are hundreds, even thousands, of different ways organizations and leaders can reinforce each of them in their own institutions.

And herein lies the power of the four C's model. There are many ways to create organizational clarity, establish consistency, add celebration, or build charity. What may work to create clarity for one company may not work for another. Or what works in establishing consistency in one industry may be very different from what is required in another. Or how one leader shows charity may be distinct from how another one does it. Very different leaders and organizations have found great success, not because they've done things exactly the same, but because they've established each element of the four C's model in their own unique ways.

By applying the model through focusing on establishing each element of it, leaders and organizations can create amazing company cultures that transform results.

Let's take a cursory overview of each element in the model.

Clarity

The first step in the model is where leaders should first focus their time, energy, and resources: creating clarity. Specifically, they should focus on creating clarity around their mission (or purpose), their values, and their vision (the eventual contribution they hope to make to the world).

Making things as clear as possible throughout their organization will establish a solid foundation for the rest of their culture to be built on. Without this base, confusion, misalignment, and even an increase in workplace drama can derail satisfaction and results. When clarity is established, it builds unity. For these reasons, clarity is the essential foundation to a great company culture. Without this solid footing, an organization's culture will never stand tall.

The most common mistake leaders and organizations make when it comes to creating clarity is believing they have been clear when the reality is they haven't been. This makes sense since many studies have shown that people need to hear and receive the same message at least seven times before they begin to understand it, internalize it, and believe it.

Most of us don't like to repeat ourselves that often; however, repetition is the key to success in establishing the clarity needed to build a strong culture. In fact, the best company cultures are created by leaders and organizations that repeat the most important messages often.

Though it is the first step in the model and should take the primary focus in the beginning, creating clarity has no finish line. It should be a never-ending pursuit for all leaders and all organizations. The more organizational clarity you create, especially around your mission, vision, and values, the stronger your foundation for a high-performing culture will be.

Consistency

The second step in the model is to establish consistency. Once a sufficient amount of organizational clarity has been created, leaders should then turn more of their attention and efforts toward consistency.

Consistency creates stability and trust within an organization. Without a high level of consistency, people will feel like they are on unsteady ground or that things are too unpredictable.

But how do you establish consistency in a rapidly changing world?

Leaders and organizations can focus on being consistent with things within their control, such as their actions, words, attitudes, systems, and approaches. They can also reinforce consistency through establishing clear schedules, expectations, and standards. Regardless of all the changes that will take place within a company, there should always be a consistent cadence with consistent practices people can count on. With the right focus on consistency, people will feel they can depend on their organization and their leaders, even in the midst of changes.

Consistency is also strengthened by traditions and norms in the workplace. These organizational habits create a company's own unique way of doing business and add to feelings of security and belonging.

When people feel secure at work, when they know at some level what to expect day in and day out, week in and week out, year in and year out, they are more likely to stay.

The key to consistency is discipline. It doesn't happen on its own without a conscious effort and focus. Leaders and organizations must make a commitment to establishing and maintaining consistency if they hope to build a great company culture.

Celebration

Once a healthy level of clarity and consistency is established, the third and final step in the model is celebration. Celebration is a combination of fun, recognition, and measurement.

Once a leader or an organization gets to this point in the model, then the fun really begins (both literally and figuratively). Research has shown human beings are wired to connect when they are having fun. For this reason, celebration is important to fostering real relationships in the workplace. When people feel connected through shared experiences that are both fun and memorable, they will want to be together and not let each other down. These strong connections help foster a strong culture.

In addition to fun, celebration is also about recognition. All human beings have a fundamental need to be recognized and appreciated. Lack of recognition will have an impact on the motivation, engagement, and satisfaction of your team. A big part of celebration is consistently and frequently recognizing others.

The last important piece of celebration is measurement. Measuring progress toward goals and making that progress super clear will allow a leader and organization ample opportunities to celebrate and recognize performance at work.

Celebration should not only happen when big goals are met. Rather, leaders should celebrate progress and even small wins along the way. When times are tough, leaders ought to find creative ways to celebrate even little wins if necessary. And in both the good times and the bad, leaders should look for simple ways to celebrate their teams daily.

This is the biggest mistake leaders and organizations make with celebration—they don't celebrate enough.

Charity

Charity is the last element of the model, but it is not the last step. In fact, it is not a step at all. The reason is that charity should be displayed, given, and expressed throughout the entire process. For this reason, it encircles the other three elements in the model.

Charity is all about helping people feel cared about and known at work. When people don't feel like anyone knows them at work or, even worse, when they feel like no one cares about them, work becomes miserable. This is true even when the person is working in a dream job or one they believed they would love.

It is really hard to walk away from a leader or organization you feel cares about you. It is really easy to walk away from a company or leader who you believe does not.

When people feel known, respected, and cared for at work, their ability and desire to be productive and to give their best becomes instinctive. When people feel unappreciated, disrespected, and not known, their performance will always be less than what it otherwise could be.

Charity is a multiplier of the other three C's within the model. Without it, the initial three C's will only go so far. With high levels of it, the other three C's will create an amazing culture that will truly transform results. The multiplying effect of charity is real.

Sometimes, well-intentioned leaders misunderstand charity and believe it encourages them to avoid confrontation or taking action on poor performance. In other words, the thought is that charity encourages leaders not to hold people accountable in the name of being kind. This couldn't be further from the truth.

First, not helping people perform well and ignoring their mistakes are not acts of kindness. They simply set people up for failure, which is unkind.

Second, a leader can perform any act with or without charity. A leader can celebrate with or without charity, they can discipline a team member with or without charity, and they can even provide clarity with or without charity. It is

245

not about the action itself, but rather how you perform that action. It's when a leader acts with charity that the impact of the actions taken will result in the most favorable outcomes, independent of the actions themselves.

Will charity make everything perfect? Of course not. When you act with charity, will people never get upset or feel slighted, unhappy, or disgruntled? Of course not. But charity will keep those negative emotions and feelings to a minimum, and this will benefit the leader and the organization.

The key to charity is sincerity. You really have to care. People can tell whether charity exists in an organization or not. You can't fake it.

The Four *C*'s

The four *C*'s work together and build on each other. Each element is important. If one or two are lacking, the culture will suffer. Combined, they create an extremely high-performing culture and produce incredible results.

As illustrated throughout the fable by Grace and her team, there are plans, actions, and systems leaders can put into place to help strengthen and establish each of the four *C*'s. In fact, leaders must put specific systems in place to reinforce each *C* if they want to build a superior culture that gets superior results.

Remember, anything you do to create clarity, consistency, celebration, and charity will help your culture improve. Likewise, anything you do that takes away or diminishes clarity, consistency, celebration, or charity will hurt your culture and, eventually, your results.

Whether you are a frontline supervisor, run your own small business, are in charge of a large division, or lead an entire corporation, applying the four *C*'s model will help you become a successful leader.

Final Word

There is tremendous satisfaction in building an exceptional company culture using the four C's model. Though Grace and her team used the model to help them transform a struggling operation, the model can also be used to elevate and accelerate an already-strong operation.

The reality is that any leader and any organization, regardless of their previous successes, can improve performance through more strongly establishing each of the four C's in the model throughout their organization.

For all leaders, this should be both reassuring and encouraging.

Acknowledgments

In writing this book, I've realized how many "Wisdom Stories" I've had the privilege to witness, learn about, or be a part of. For this reason, first and foremost, I'd like to recognize and thank all those leaders who have used the tried-and-true leadership principles found in the four C's model. Thank you for shaping the work experiences of millions of people and for creating a better working world.

Next, my wife, Lisa, has always been and continues to be an unwavering source of encouragement and support. Your kind truth and feedback always make my work so much better.

My five children have also been very supportive throughout this process. Much of my writing has been done during the unprecedented coronavirus pandemic, which has forced many changes in our lives including having all my children home from school all day. Thank you for allowing me to spend time on my book and, most importantly, spend extra time with you during this unique time in our lives.

I would be remiss if I didn't thank the several editors, designers, and others who have helped with the creation of this book. Your own personal touch and improvements have been invaluable.

I need to thank God for His matchless love, steady hand, and gentle guidance in my life. Thank you for your many blessings and the gift of life. I feel the love you have for me and for all your children on Earth.

Finally, to all those I have had the privilege and honor to work alongside throughout my career. To name all of you would be completely impossible, but you know who you are, and I am forever grateful for you. Thank you for teaching me so much!

About the Author

Tim Burningham is an experienced leader and former CEO in the health care industry. He and the organizations he has led have received multiple awards for outstanding performance including being recognized as a top 100 Skilled Nursing and Rehabilitation Center by U.S. News and World Report. Tim has created high-performing company cultures everywhere he's worked, which has led to remarkable results.

Currently, Tim is President of The Center for Company Culture, a management consulting firm committed to helping organizations and leaders build cohesive teams and create amazing company cultures. His practical and straightforward approach has assisted leaders and organizations across the world to improve performance and love what they do. He is a sought-after speaker, guest lecturer, consultant, and executive coach.

Tim lives in the Houston area with his wife, Lisa, and their five children.

To learn more about Tim and the Center for Company Culture, please visit www.TheCenterforCompanyCulture.com or connect with him on LinkedIn.

251

The Center for Company Culture

The Center for Company Culture is dedicated to helping organizations accelerate their results through effective leadership and creating a high-performing company culture. We follow a proven system to help companies implement and follow the four *C*'s model. To learn more about our services, please visit our website at

TheCenterforCompanyCulture.com.

For more information about the four *C*'s model, please contact Tim at

Tim@TheCenterforCompanyCulture.com.

You can also find free resources and tools to help you apply the four *C*'s model at

https://TheCenterforCompanyCulture.com/free-tools.

The Center for Company Culture has also created an online course to help leaders learn how to create their own high-peforming company culture at their own pace from the comfort and safety of their home or office. You can learn more at

TheCenterforCompanyCulture.thinkific.com.

www.ingramcontent.com/pod-product-compliance
Lightning Source LLC
Chambersburg PA
CBHW070527220526
45467CB00003B/892